Journey
of the
Awakened
Psychic

Joe Gacoscos

When I run after what I think I want, my days are a furnace of stress and anxiety; if I sit in my own place of patience, what I need flows to me, and without pain. From this I understand that what I want also wants me, is looking for me and attracting me. There is a great secret here for anyone who can grasp it.

—RUMI

Author: Joe Gacoscos
Cover designed by Joe Gacoscos

Book website: www.MyPsychicAwakening.com
My Psychic Awakening Academy with Joe Gacoscos

Printed in the United States of America

First Printing: Aug 2018
Difference Press

ISBN-13: 978-1-7180884-7-4

To my family...Who always encouraged me to be "not like the others" me.

TABLE OF CONTENTS

FOREWORD

THE PLANET GIVES BIRTH to more and more gifted souls each day. You may have heard of these light warriors. Perhaps you are one. These light warriors include empaths, intuitives, psychics, mediums, Starseeds, indigos, crystal and rainbow children.

Many of these gifted souls are in the midst of their psychic awakening. Sadly, though, many of these people are trapped in a spiritual closet. They don't dare come out. They fear the thought of being labeled crazy, weird, or not normal.

Rather than expressing their gifts, what do these gifted souls do instead? They hide. They try to suppress their abilities. They grow up believing they're not normal. They continue hiding in the shadows.

What's the price of staying hidden in this spiritual closet?

Many feel like they can't be expressive of who their true selves. Some become ill—mentally, emotionally and physically. Others experience overwhelm from their abilities. Spirits, beings or entities haunt them in their dreams. They feel like a prisoner in their own skin.

Even worse, many grow up with the trauma of psychological misdiagnosis. Families feel helpless to assist their "strange kid".

While all the above are true, here's where this becomes a real crisis: The world misses out on what should be a shining light from each one of these souls. Each of these souls miss out on the next steps of their spiritual evolution. Each misses out on an opportunity to be of service to others.

This is why I wrote *Journey of the Awakened Psychic.* In my own awakening, I see there are many who are still in the shadows searching for some way out. Many need simple validation. Others seek a lifeline from overwhelm–or worse.

Seeking answers along your psychic awakening journey? Looking to make sense of your supernatural experiences? Need help from being overwhelmed with foreign energies? If you answer "yes" to any of these questions, then this book is especially written for you.

This book helps you navigate the journey to awakening your psychic gifts. You are taken on a journey of <u>ten steps</u> to honing your psychic abilities. From leaning to ground, to healing your chakras, to reading and healing, and to learning to manifest via powerful psychic energies. This book has something for everyone. From novice to advanced practitioner, all awakening light warriors benefit. And in particular for the challenges of the naturally gifted, this guide is for you.

By picking up this book, I know this isn't exactly a "normal" decision. Thus, that you entrust me for this part of your life's path is not one I take lightly. Rather, my intent is that you learn to embrace who you really are. Embrace your gifts. Embrace the very reason for being born on this planet.

That said, may you enjoy the spiritual awakening of your third eye, the insights, and inspiration many other awakening students have enjoyed as you journey forward.

Many blessings,
<u>Joe Gacoscos</u>
My Psychic Awakening Academy

P.S. Are your psychic abilities waking up? Watch this video I filmed on the beach. See if you can relate!:

MyPsychicAwakening.com/welcome.

JOE'S VIDEO INTRO

By Joe Gacoscos

PRELUDE: SEEING BEYONG THE VEIL

Throughout history, the Gifted have been suppressed.

What do I mean by this?

While it might seem like I'm exaggerating, tap deep into your own intuition about what you're going to read...

To put it mildly, the gifted probably make up 1% of society today. They see and sense things mere mortals can't even dream of accessing.

When this happens, they're thought of as crazy. Insane. *Different.*

Why? Why is it that those that are born different – even supernatural – are thought of this way?

It's because we have access to what others don't.

And that is, TRUTH.

Pause for a moment to let that sink in.

Imagine for a moment being able to see beyond "the veil".

What do I mean by the *veil*? I describe the veil as kind of a hypnosis that's surrounding the planet that all this psychic stuff, or even spirituality in general, isn't real.

The fact of the matter is, many are indeed having VERY REAL experiences.

It can be anything from seeing signs like 333, 777, or 11:11 and getting messages that way.

Or it's getting premonitions about earthquakes or other significant events *before* they happen.

Or it's getting messages from the "other side" – from Angels, Ascended Masters, or even from people who have already passed away.

~~~

What's on the other side?

What information, message, or insight found there?

Even further, what if the veil itself is an illusion?

Here's the thing about Truth (Truth with a capital "T")...

Truth is Truth – Meaning it's immovable, unquestionable, deeply rooted...

Here are a few examples:

It's that feeling you get when you bask in the glow of a beautiful sunset. The Truth is, it's just *feels* beautiful. Full stop. Nothing to argue about here!

It's staring at the beauty of blue ocean waves crashing against the shoreline. It can literally leave you breathless. It feels like time is standing still. That's Truth.

It's being present to nature's glory when you stare at majestic mountains, breathe in that crisp morning air, and watch the sun as it rises in the background.

You feel like you're in the presence of a force greater than any of us.

That "greater force" or that greater "thing" – That's Truth.

~~~

Here's the thing about Truth:

You can't argue with it. People, friends, enemies, colleagues all can't argue. Unless you really are just a disagreeable person, there's nothing left to say when something is just True.

By Joe Gacoscos

If it's beautiful, it's beautiful, right?

For some people, though, to take a quote from the movie *A Few Good Men*, "You can't handle the Truth!"

Here's why Truth it's hard to handle for some people, especially when it comes to your higher psychic knowing...

When you finally do come into these GREATER Truths, in a way, this is what True Spiritual Awakening is all about, is it not?

The whole basis for a spiritual awakening IS <u>seeing beyond the veil</u>.

And when you see beyond the veil, how you live your life, the choices you make, the people you hang around with – ALL of that <u>shifts</u>.

Here's what people don't realize, though, about any kind of spiritual awakening...

People think that Spiritual Awakening is all love and light and roses.

Well, I don't want to put a damper on things here but here's what's to consider...

Prior to gaining this new level of Truth, consider, what if how you *were* living is based on an illusion? A lie? Or even based on societal agreements that aren't even reality-based, but mere convenience?

Consider that when parents would say that in order to be successful, for example, you need to be a Doctor when you grow up.

Is that true?

Plenty of people are successful otherwise!

And yet, how many of us are now living *someone else's truth.*

Where in your own life have you bought into an illusion? Believing in what you *thought* was true? Only to be disappointed...

Listen the Truth hurts. Many times it's painful realization.

That *realization*, however... That's but the <u>beginning</u> of your Awakening.

As the saying goes, it's The Truth that shall set you Free.
And who wouldn't want freedom, right?

~ ~ ~

So you might be asking, "Joe, what does all this have to do with the Gifted being suppressed?"

Consider this:

When you have your Spiritual Awakening via the Truths your psychic gifts give you access to, you in essence break away from the norms set by society.

You break away from the herd.

And when you break away, you stand out.

You ARE *different*.

When you are different, society has a way of wanting to reel you back in, right?

Until others have their own awakening, however, fortunately or unfortunately, here's the new reality:

You can't *undo* seeing the Truth.

You can't undo how a deep Truth feels.

You can't undo your newfound taste of Freedom.

And no one can take away your psychic and intuitive *access* to these higher spiritual Truths once you get a taste of it!

~ ~ ~

A word of caution about any kind of spiritual or psychic awakening.

It can be lonely.

It can even be scary.

By Joe Gacoscos

A psychic awakening can be especially scary because of what you now have access to – messages from Spirit, premonitions, or getting weird signs like 333, 777, 11:11.

For many awakening psychics, yes, you're getting these "downloads" of information from the *other side*, but you're stuck wondering, "What does it mean?"

For many of you, these experiences are random at best. You wish you had a way of controlling your abilities.

You wish you were able to access these Truths more on demand, and at will.

Because you are different – part of that 1% – who is there really to turn to when you have questions? Who can help guide you through this *unique* kind of spiritual awakening? What do you do when you're confused about what steps to take next?

It's no wonder why we seek out a psychic for a reading, right!?!

To help you answer these pressing questions is why I wrote this book, *The Journey of the Awakened Psychic: The 10-Step Guide on How to Open Your Third Eye.*

I know for many of you, learning to control your abilities is but the first step!

For many of you, you intuitive just know that you can then use your gifts to even help others see beyond the veil so that they, too, can access their Truth.

You want to help others. You want to heal others. And you know deep down that by helping others heal, you heal.

~ ~ ~

Consider this now on a more societal and planetary level.

What happens when more and more people access these greater spiritual Truths? What happens when more people see beyond the veil? What happens to society as a whole as it heals from this hypnosis?

Personally, I believe that we are amidst a great awakening happening on the planet right now.

Consider that information used to only be available to "the chosen".

Now anyone can simply go on YouTube for information on how to meditate!

The more people that wake up, the more the need for guides to help people out of the darkness, to pass through that veil, and then to help to navigate through the light.

Consider that if YOU are reading this, perhaps you are one of those "chosen" guides, born to help others. You are a way-shower to help others access their Truth.

And when you learn to access and hone that mythical 3rd eye, as taught in this book, it's your 3rd eye that gives you access to these higher spiritual Truths.

By following along with this book to access your 3rd eye, you starting seeing beyond the veil more and more as you journey through each of the 10 steps.

Simply by following along in this book, and accessing the "Awaken Your Psychic Gifts in 7 Days Mini-Challenge", you have all the foundational tools necessary.

~ ~ ~

It is my sincere hope that as you gain access to these greater spiritual Truths that you use them in the pursuit of something good. Something noble. Something that will *raise your own vibration as well as others* in the process.

I do believe the energy you put out is the energy you get back.

By Joe Gacoscos

Just know that my intention for writing this book is to not only answer your questions about how to hone your psychic gifts...

It's also so that you in turn use your gifts for some greater good.

Whether you want to use your gifts to help heal others, or simply use your 3rd eye to make better professional or life decisions, just know that the possibilities are endless!

You need not be suppressed nor scared anymore.

Enjoy your *different* and your *crazy*.

May you be blessed as you journey along with this book.

Blessings,
Joe Gacoscos

CHAPTER 1 – CAUGHT BETWEEN TWO WORLDS

I T'S A WARM SUNNY SAN DIEGO DAY when the office phone rings. I answer, "Hi, this is Joe of My Psychic Awakening Academy, how may I..." A woman's voice interrupts my customary greeting.

"Are you Joe? The spiritual teacher and healer Joe?" she asks softly yet with a sense of urgency.

I reply, "Yes, this is Joe. How can I help..."

Her soft voice cuts in, "Hi Joe. I read through everything on your website. I swear it was like you were speaking directly to me! I'm calling because I'd like to know when's your earliest availability so you can help me."

In her rush, she remembers to state, "Sorry. I'm Joann by the way."

Normally people take time to ease into a conversation. This is atypical—and I come across lots of not-so-typical things in my practice! I take a small pause.

"Hi Joann. It sounds really urgent. May I ask, how is it that you believe I can help you? What on my website did you read that called out to you exactly?"

She hesitates as if she's about to cry.

"I feel so stupid for even saying this out loud. Don't laugh." Her voice trails.

"I see dead people. And I see them, like, all the time."

"Ah, I see," I say compassionately.

"Sometimes I see spirit guides and angels. Sometimes I see these entities, too. And sometimes those ones aren't so nice. Those ones are scary if I'm being really honest."

Her voice trembles, "Sometimes they're there at the edge of my bed, like they want to speak to me."

She continues, "Joe, I'm not crazy—at least I'd like to believe that I'm not! You know, I'm a professional woman. I work as a paralegal in a high-powered law firm. People respect the work that I do.

"I wonder to myself sometimes, 'If I'm a professional, intelligent woman, then why can't I get these weird experiences under control?'

"I literally lay awake in bed at night, staring at the ceiling. I'm hoping and praying that tonight's the night I finally find some peace.

"Furthermore," she continues, "I wonder what this will do to my kids? One of my kids seems like she's turning out just like me. I need to learn how to get this under control...

"Sorry, I'm rambling," she says, attempting to ease the tension with an uneasy giggle. "As you can tell, I'm a so overwhelmed. I don't know where else to turn."

As she's speaking, I take a moment and close my eyes. I take a quick psychic look at her energy.

"It looks like you have many beings around you," I share with her. "When looking at your space, I can only imagine it's really overwhelming for you."

"Oh my gosh! You can see them, too? Well, of course, you're a psychic..." she lets out a small laugh.

She continues, "Yes, overwhelming for sure. It's like all this energy, all these messages, and all at once! Some days, it's like sure, it's cool to talk to some of these spirits. But other days…"

"Let me guess, you just can't seem to turn it off?" I ask.

"Yes! Exactly!"

She continues, "I searched all over the internet for answers. I read some Esther Hicks books. I even watched a bunch of YouTube videos."

"How did those help you?" I ask.

"Not so much. There are many great videos out there that tell you what to do. However, I don't get the feedback if I'm doing this right. No matter what I try, I still keep seeing these spirits all around.

"I pray a lot. I even went to church for help on what to do. The priest was really nice. But I felt like he could only go so far.

"Friends would try to help. But all I would get from them is, 'Oh, Joann, you're just probably imagining things'.

"My mom, bless her. Throughout my childhood she was scared for me. For a while, she thought I was possessed. Growing up I saw her feeling helpless sometimes. The best she could help me with was, 'Joann, you'll outgrow it eventually.'

"I pray I won't do that to my own kids."

She sighs. I sigh with her.

"How was it for you growing up?" I ask.

"When I was in my teens, I learned to ignore it," she says. "Or I just kept praying and praying. It would go away for a little bit, but it seemed like these psychic senses were always there in the background.

"The older I got, I'm in my late 30's now, the more I couldn't suppress it anymore.

"I do have some friends who are more open-minded. They try to cheer me up. 'You have a gift!' I feel like it is a gift sometimes. But I feel like, if it's such a gift, then why does it feel like such a curse?

"Gifts shouldn't feel like a curse."

Through mounting tears, I hear her say, "I can't do this on my own anymore. Joe, I'm a highly educated woman, you know? I have college degree. I know I'm not crazy. I feel like there's no one really to talk to about this...

"I need to make sense of all these crazy psychic experiences. I really need to learn how to control this. I feel like if I can take control of these abilities, then I can take back control of my life.

"Can you help me?"

I ask her to take a deep breath. She inhales a deep breath in, more than she'd allowed herself it seems in a long time. Even I could feel her release of tension as she exhales.

"Yes, this is why I'm here Joann. I help gifted people like you to know they indeed are not crazy. How about we set a time for an initial breakthrough session? We'll drill down a bit on your challenges. We'll uncover solutions to your specific challenges. How does that sound?"

Relieved, she replies, "Yes. I would like that."

YOU'RE TOO OPEN

When people like Joann come to see me, their psychic senses are completely open. To give an analogy, it's like her psychic senses are an antenna. It's an overactive antenna that's tuned in to every single radio station. All at the same time. One that never turns off.

In Joann's case, it sounds great that she can experience these psychic phenomena. The problem is this ability has her experiencing too much energy all at once.

In getting to know Joann better, I learn she is like many others who I work with. She encounters all kinds of psychic experiences:

- She *sees* beings and entities in her dreams
- She *hears* messages from dead relatives
- More than just empathy, she *feels deeply* the energies and emotions of other people
- She would somehow *know* ahead of time about major events including mass shootings or major earthquakes
- Premonitions are the worst—she feels guilty not being able to tell anyone about them

Of course, not everyone who comes to see me is as psychically open as Joann. I often get people who come in for more simple psychic experiences. They might ask, "Joe, is it weird that think of someone, then 5 minutes later, that person calls me?" I laugh, "Welcome to my world!"

No matter where you fall on the spectrum of abilities, there a few camps people tend to fall into:

- Fear that they can't control these abilities
- That *something* will control them
- Many times, it's fear they will lose control all together

In the case of Joann, she lives in terror because she feels she can't control her abilities. It's as if everywhere she turns, the abilities have taken control of her life.

Furthermore, those who need help often feel there are not very many people to talk to about this subject. Growing up, they try to suppress their abilities so as not to stand out. The more they try to suppress, however, the more they feel like a pressure cooker waiting to burst.

In essence, people with what are supposed to be gifts feel out of control. They experience fear, overwhelm, and loss of self-expression. At worst, they feel alone. Many are high-powered professionals with high visibility jobs. Yet, they feel they must hide, even in plain view.

Often, I will hear some variation on this question: "If these psychic abilities are a gift, why do they feel like such a curse?"

Gift versus curse. They feel caught between two worlds. They're looking for a pathway out.

A SEARCH FOR CERTAINTY

By reading this book, there's no doubt that you, too, are searching for answers. When it comes to this world of psychic phenomena, ask yourself the following:

- What inexplicable psychic experiences have you had?
- Perhaps you see auras or spirits?
- You hear messages from guardian angels?
- More than simply empathizing, you can *feel* what others feel?
- Perhaps you channeled some energy. Afterwards you thought to yourself, "Was that me that just said those words?"

Like you, thousands of people are scouring the internet searching for credible information. As of this writing, when you Google "psychic", the search engine returns over 21,800,000 results! With millions of search results available, you're asking yourself,

"Who do I trust?"

"Where do I turn?"

"What sources are legitimate?"

Some of you have gone to churches, counselors, and psychologists. I've had multiple clients tell me they pray. A lot! They hope God gives them guidance.

Helping you break down barriers to your psychic awakening is the purpose of this book. Realize that not only did you find this book, **this book found you.** Resonate in anyway with anything you have read thus far? If so, encourage you to take time to soak in the information on the pages that follow. Allow the words to flow through you. In so doing, the answers you seek shall also find you.

I encourage you to pour through the meditations, exercises, and insights on the pages that follow. My goal is you feel validated in your experiences. While you may experience overwhelm or fear now, this book provides you a different pathway. Unless you feel otherwise, there's no need to remain scared and stuck between two worlds. There is a way out. There is a way to overcome. There is better way to be in control.

BOOK OVERVIEW

This book takes you on a journey of discovery. Each chapter devotes a major step in awakening your psychic third eye. You learn to ground each step before moving onto the next. While you can power your way through this book, please consider the following:

Each of the steps is meant as a progression of embodying the information. Keep in mind, it's one thing to know something as an intellectual exercise. It's quite another to have this information sink in to your body, to the depths of your soul.

As you journey through, each chapter contains step-by-step meditations. This progression leads you through:

1. Learning more about your abilities
2. To honing your natural gifts
3. To activating your third eye to perform a basic reading or healing
4. To elevating these gifts to help you perform even greater levels of energy work
5. Learning to avoid pitfalls along the way
6. Experiencing a new kind of spiritual awakening with your gifts

If you are anything like, me, you'll want to skip ahead. Keep in mind, though, this is a journey! You gain *more* by taking some time to <u>slow down</u>. Allow the energy of each step to permeate into the depths of your being. As you journey through the rest of this book, you can always refer to past chapters as stand-alone lessons.

Remember that many of the answers you seek are already within you. This book helps you access them. Dedicate the time. My promise is what arises will be beyond anything you can now comprehend. Pleasant surprises are in store for those who commit to this journey.

BOOK FORMAT

From novice to advanced practitioner, there is something in this book for everyone. As you continue through the material, what I recommend is you take anywhere from 30-minutes to one hour to get through one chapter. Then, allow that information to soak in overnight. While reading, find a dedicated meditation spot made only for you during this time.

Each chapter will contain the following 3 easy-to-follow elements:

1. An explanation on a topic, concept, and/or tool
2. A story of one of my clients or students to illustrate an example
3. A guided meditation for you to follow

It's as simple as that: Follow each of the 3 mini-steps in each chapter and move onto the next chapter.

Now if you really want to ingrain all these teachings, practice the meditations at least three times. You will gain even more insights and a-ha's each time you meditate. Many even report receiving direct messages from Source each time they meditate. You won't want to miss out on that!

I also encourage you to keep a journal. This is so you can look back on you're a-ha's and insights from each chapter.

AVOID THIS TRAP

Before moving on, I'd like to point out two specific worlds. Embracing one world helps you. The other world hurts you. The latter world of hurt is the trap to which many fall prey.

The first world is the world of *experience*. Explore the answers to these questions:

- What's the difference between reading about riding a bike versus actually going out and riding?
- What's the difference between sitting on the couch watching a workout video versus actually going to the gym and exercising up a sweat?
- What's the difference between hearing about the benefits of meditating versus actually sitting down to meditate for an hour yourself?

As you can see, the difference is clear: Experience. You gain much more when you are in the acts of doing, embodying, and gaining wisdom you can feel. You feel the difference down to your bones.

With the second world, this is the "knowing about" world. In my coaching practice, there have been so many times where I hear clients say, "I already *know* all that Joe!" My response: "Great! You know about meditating, but how often are you actually taking the time to meditate? How many times per week? How many hours?"

The realization sinks in. It's no wonder why there is real change. There's no *practice.*

You *can* breeze through this book. You may already "know" about the tools. You may have already tried out these techniques from other teachers. Yet, are you someone who has practiced? Embodied? Mastered?

Avoid the "knowing about" trap. Don't be that person. Continue being in the mindset of learning instead. Take this opportunity to give yourself the *experience* of mastery. This book helps you takes those steps.

A COMPANION E-COURSE FOR YOUR JOURNEY

My goal for all readers of my book is that you truly ingrain what you learn. In other words, you go beyond just *reading about* the steps – you actually GO THROUGH AND EXPERIENCING the steps.

To help you experience actually awakening your 3rd eye, I have a special surprise for you! By being a reader of this book, you get an **instant access** when you sign up for my video e-course called the

"Awaken Your Psychic Gifts in 7 Days Challenge". **This mini e-course** contains many of the guided meditations found in this book.

Each day of this Bootcamp, I release mini-training videos you can watch anywhere, any time, and in only 20-30 minutes per day. With me as you guide, you gradually open your psychic third eye in a grounded, step-by-step manner.

While it doesn't contain all of the meditations in the book, the bootcamp gives you just what you need to give your very first psychic reading. Imagine giving your first energy reading 7 DAYS from now! You learn the bare basics to really jumpstart your way to psychic success.

Additionally, you also get a chance to access a student-only membership. As you go through this bootcamp, you can post any of your questions as you go through the meditations. Additionally, you're surrounded by like-minded people going through the exact same journey you are going through.

For many of the clients I work with, it can't be understated how this awakening journey is a big deal. While this 7-Day Bootcamp is not necessary, it's my way of giving you that extra motivation to help give you the jumpstart you need. Click the bootcamp link above to sign up in seconds. It's easy to sign up. It's the perfect companion to reading this book!

You're likely excited to get onto the actual energy tools and the ten steps of the journey. Before we get to that awesome material, allow me to first share my story so you get a sense of who I am and how we can relate.

By Joe Gacoscos

CHAPTER 2 – MY AWAKENING STORY

FLASHING BACK TO 1989, I grow up in a modest, suburban, middle-class home located near San Francisco. My childhood is quite average. I grow up without any kind of trauma, abuse or neglect. My parents never put me on any heavy medications. Unfortunately, I hear this from people I help all the time about their childhoods. Thank goodness, mine is relatively normal.

While my childhood isn't very tumultuous, there is one story that *is* most out of the ordinary. When I was a pre-teen, I remember waking up in the middle of the night. I wake up to see blue numbers flashing "2:00" on my digital alarm clock. As I look up from the clock, my eyes stare up to a black void on the ceiling above me.

As I stare at this dark space, I see a glow of heavenly light start to fade in. I glimpse around. Might it be a car's headlights flashing through the window? I check. The curtains are shut. There's no way moving headlights could cause that specific kind of a heavenly glow anyway.

I gaze even more intently on the space above. The glow begins to fade. I try to make it come back, but it is already gone.

Although that heavenly glow disappears, I am left with a strong and clear message:

Your grandmother just died.

Now mind you, my grandmother is located halfway around the world in the Philippines.

While the vision itself isn't scary, the next revelation is. I wake up later that morning to hear the sad news:

"Joe, your grandma died last night."

I'm beside myself. I think, "How could I have possibly known this?"

It's in that moment I become scared.

I whisper to no one, "There's no way. I'm not sharing this with anybody."

It's in this subconscious moment I decide to shut these abilities off. I can ignore them...or so it would seem...

IGNORANT BLISS

From the time of my grandmother's passing and into my teen years, I have similar psychic experiences. These experiences aren't as vivid. This is because I'd decided in my younger years to shut these abilities off. I do a good job trying to ignore these "psychic hits" most of the time. However, as I would later learn, Spirit tries its hardest to get our attention anyway.

As an example, street lights would flash off as I walk or drive by. Whether on the west coast, east coast, or even being in the Navy stationed in Italy, street lights would turn off. Each time, I think to myself, "weird!" Then I dismiss it. In the back of my mind, though, I suspect it's a guardian angel with a message. I brush these off. I chalk these up to coincidence instead. I stick to my childhood decision of trying to ignore them.

In another example, my dad starts sharing at the dinner table. "One of the people working for me is having behavior problems," he says.

As my dad continues his story, I could *feel* what his coworker is feeling. I start getting this strong intuitive sense. Keep in mind, I'm barely a teenager hearing this story. I have no real-life experience to know any better.

I nonchalantly reply, "I think he's having problems at home."

My dad looks at me, "How did you know that? Wow, you are very wise. As a matter of fact, yes, he is having marriage problems."

I continue having these kinds of intuitive and psychic experiences growing up. I learn while my senses are normal for me, they are not normal for everyone else. I buy into, like my dad states, I am just "wise".

Ignorance is bliss!

Even still, I decide not to share my experiences with many people as I get older.

THE TRANSITION

Fast forward from my teens to a summer day in 2009. At this point, I'm well into my thirties.

I'm trying to get over a heavy-duty relationship breakup. A friend of mine says, "There's something you have to know, Joe…

"However long you were in a relationship," he says, "take half of that. That's usually how long it'll take for you to get over your relationship."

In disbelief, I reply, "Oh, hell no! I ain't got time! I want to move on with my life!"

By this point, I'm very deep into exploring change-work and spirituality. These include meditation, Advaita, non-duality, sitting in Satsangs, Neuro-Linguistic Programming (NLP), and even Zen Buddhism.

With meditation, I learn about the "Oneness". The experience is one of vastness. I experience the word-less *all and the nothing* many spiritual traditions teach. I learn to take my everyday consciousness beyond space and time. At that time in my life, meditating like this helps me to escape the pain of the breakup. Still, I feel a need for something more...tangible.

To speed up my progress, I decide to find a spiritually-based therapist. I seek one who blends the spiritual with the practical. I find a great therapist with a Tibetan Buddhist background.

Working with her is like sitting in front of a Buddhist master each week. I learn to get so deep in the meditation, much deeper than when I would practice on my own. I become more and more one with the everything and the nothing. It's a state of pure bliss.

Along with therapy, she also helps me open up to the *energy* side of meditation. As I meditate with her, any boundaries just melt away. Old energy blocks disappear. At the same time, I feel an energetic rush.

For nearly a year I meditate this way almost every day straight. Sometimes I sit for hours in meditation. As a result, I become even more sensitive to different kinds of energies. This is especially true for sensing spiritual energies.

During one session, we come out of one of her wonderful guided meditations. She asks me how I'm progressing with the relationship stuff. I tell her it's better, but still feeling a little stuck. It feels like an energy that's trapped deep inside.

From the therapy side of things, she suspects this energy has to do with my father. During one session, she brings up how our fathers play a role in our relationships. Little do I know this would open the door for what happens next...

THE PIVOTAL MOMENT

So there we are, chatting in her peaceful, Zen inspired office. Next thing you know, while I see her mouth move, all I hear is "mwah-mwah-mwah-mwah." It sounds like the teacher in the *Charlie Brown* cartoons.

In vain I try to refocus on reality. Instead, I begin seeing this swirl of light above her head. It intensifies. It grows. Later I would realize it's just like the glow of light I saw on my dark ceiling decades ago. The difference is this is now in broad daylight. It looks as if space and time are bending in on itself about two feet above her. In that moment, my body freezes.

The mwah-mwah-mwah's fade away even though I see her lips still move up and down. The swirl of heavenly light opens up more and more. It's nearly as large as the couch she's seated on. In a curious mix of panic and calm, I wonder,

Can she not see this? Am I the only one? She's still acting pretty normal, as if nothing is going on...

In the next moment, I manage to interrupt her. With the swirling still up above her, I ask, "So how was it growing up with your father?"

Was that my voice? Did I just ask her that?

With my body still frozen, I hear her say, "I was a challenging teenager. It affected my relationship with my dad. It's how I eventually became a therapist."

The swirling light intensifies.

I respond, "For some reason, I feel compelled to tell you this...Your dad says he's proud of you and he loves you."

Who said that? Obviously, I said that. But where did that come from? How would I even know that? What the...?

A tear starts to roll down her cheek. I hear her whisper "thank you" as she quickly tries to regain her composure.

No sooner does the tear fall off her chin that I see the mysterious swirl fade away. As easily as it came, the swirl disappears into the ether. It feels like I can move my body again. My therapist carries on about fathers.

In that moment, my world turns upside down.

THE SHIFT

It seems like days, weeks, and months go by after the therapist incident. My analytical brain is on overdrive. I search for answers online. I buy a couple books. Nothing satisfies my longing for answers.

Fortunately, I meet two gifted psychics within a few weeks of my therapist visit. They happen to be attending the same NLP training workshop I'm attending. We meet for dinner. Getting past my fear of others judging, I grill them both for answers.

Epiphany, the first psychic hears my story. She then asks, "How did your therapist react to your message?"

"A tear rolled down her check as soon as I said those words," I reply.

Almost nonchalantly, she says, "Good job! The message you delivered came through."

Baffled, I ask, "Umm...that's it? But how do I *control* that?"

The two psychics give each other kind of a knowing, insider look. They burst into laughter.

They then both then gaze at me. It's like they're staring deep into my soul.

Epiphany bursts out, "Joe, you're so psychic."

"Huh?" I mutter. Mind you, I hadn't ever told anyone about my childhood experience.

"You're so psychic."

She looks at the top of my head, at my crown chakra. "You *know* things. Energies come in. You have a knowingness about things."

Just like I just knew the moment my grandmother died.

Epiphany looks at my belly, at my 2nd chakra. "...and then you take that energy, and you get a *feel* for it."

I do that a lot actually. I can feel what others are going through.

Then she looks at my forehead, or my third eye. "You try to *see* the energy for yourself. But you get stuck at reading from the 2nd chakra, for how things feel."

Chakra? What's a chakra?

"The problem you run into," she says, still nonchalantly, "you can't tell the difference if it's your feelings versus the other person's feelings.

"So you get stuck in your 2nd chakra. Then you get frustrated. Then you don't sense anything at all."

Oh my gosh, how does she even know this?

"I know this because I just gave you a reading, in case you're wondering."

What the...Can she hear what I'm thinking?

I must've had the strangest look on my face. Both psychics give each other that insider look again. They giggle even more. It's like they're talking to each other telepathically.

Jenny, the other psychic at the table chimes in, "You know, Joe, I'm looking at starting my own psychic training school. Would you like to be my apprentice as I do a trial-run for my first class?"

Still in disbelief over the conversation happening at the table, I manage to mutter, "Yes." Little do I know what I am actually walking into.

As the Universe would have it, Jenny becomes my psychic and spiritual mentor.

SOAKING UP THIS NEW ENERGY

A week after my dinner with the two psychics, I start training with Jenny. In the twelve weeks that follow, I learn all I can in earnest. I'm like a sponge. I soak it all in. Some days, I meditate for hours. She teaches me a system on how to wake up my psychic abilities. These include:

- How to run my own energy and let go of other people's energies
- Proper psychic boundaries
- How to read energy
- How to give a simple healing for myself and others
- An introduction to energy work

She shows me a new way to meditate. This meditation originates from the Berkeley Psychic Institute. It's unlike the "one-with-everything" meditations. I learn a more active way to meditate.

She teaches me to own my psychic space. I learn how to create psychic boundaries where there were none before. With energy tools, I learn to release years and lifetimes of stuck energies. These tools help me to release more energy in a few sittings compared to my year in therapy.

Life as I know transforms. My outlook transforms. The way I relate to energy transforms. I can't believe how quickly my energy shifts.

As I journey through Jenny's coaching, I finally come to a moment of peace.

Many of my past questions—from childhood knowing about my grandmother's death; to being called "wise" by my father in my teens; to my therapist's father delivering a message through me as an adult—start to make sense. I gain a new a pathway towards deeper understanding. I feel peace and calm where before there was only the feeling of being incomplete.

The journey, I realize, is only beginning.

WHEN STUDENT BECOMES THE GUIDE

A few years go by and I move to San Diego. I am someone, when I get into something, I really get into it. I take more advanced Clairvoyant training. I attend a school called Intuitive Insights School of Intuition. Additionally, I regularly attend a Clairvoyant Meetup group. I practice reading and healing each week. At Intuitive Insights, I make my way through all the programs including:

- Psychic Tools
- Beginner Clairvoyance
- Advanced Clairvoyance
- Spiritual Teachers and Leaders Program
- Trance Medium Healing
- Trance Medium Channeling

Oddly enough, what I learn doesn't feel "new" to me. It feels familiar. It's like waking up to skills and abilities from many lifetimes. While clairvoyance doesn't come as easily to me at first, I ease into it. The more I get out of my own way, the more that opens up. Performing energy work and healing also feels natural. It's like it's part of my bones, like it's part of my DNA. Deep down I know this to be true.

Vessa Rinehart-Phillips, Director of Intuitive Insights, says many who come through these programs have many past lives of being a healer, teacher or psychic. Many have karma to complete. In this lifetime, they come back for even more mastery or pay back karmic debt. This makes sense to me. It explains why I feel so driven to pursue this level of energy work and spirituality.

With more mastery, people start asking me to read and heal. I open my own professional reading, healing and spiritual mentoring practice. (Check out https://www.TrueInsights.net for more background information). The mentoring caters to awakening psychics from all walks of life, which is the basis for this book.

As of the time of this writing, I also teach the Intuitive Insights School of Intuition Clairvoyant Training Programs. As much as I love to read and heal, I love to teach even more! I feel like this is my birthright to now be a guide for others who are going through the similar journey I have.

In pages that follow, you'll find I take all my experiences—

- Giving thousands of hours of lectures on intuition and psychic development
- Working with hundreds of students in awakening their psychic abilities
- Working one-on-one with hundreds of healing clients throughout the years

—and I distill it down to an easy-to-follow, proven 10 step-process which I call the *Journey of the Awakened Psychic*.

Follow these proven steps. You, too, can develop your psychic abilities in a safe and grounded manner. You overcome the challenges and pitfalls I see many students often face.

Skip the years of trying to do this on your own. Instead, shortcut your way to owning your abilities rather than your abilities owning you.

Speaking of shortcutting your way to success, have you signed up for the "Awaken Your Psychic Gifts in 7 Days Challenge" yet? If not, visit now. Sign up in seconds. You'll find bonus support material and access to extra downloads that compliment this book. Post and tag me with any of your questions to our secret Facebook™ group (use codeword TRUTH after you sign up to get in!) as you read along in this book.

Ready to find out more about the ten steps of the *Journey of the Awakened Psychic*? Jump to an overview of these ten steps in the next chapter.

CHAPTER 3 INTRO

CHAPTER 3 – UNCOVERING A BURIED TREASURE

A YOUNG WOMAN NAMED JACKIE CALLS from New York to inquire about my services. She is a professional massage therapist and a naturally gifted psychic. She is someone who is searching for answers about her energy challenges.

"How can I help you?" I ask.

"Hello, I was referred to you by another life coach. She referred me to you because she doesn't work with people like me, people with…"

She hesitates.

I chime in, "People with psychic abilities?"

Jackie laughs. "Yes. Wannabe psychics like me."

"Tell me a little bit about yourself. What had you reach out to me today?"

"Well, to be honest, I don't know where to start. I read online that I classify as 'highly sensitive'. I don't know about all that. All I know is I walk down the street, and I can see everyone's auras. I try to tune them out, thinking they can't be real. But there they are! Plain as day.

"It's even worse when I'm working with my massage clients. Along with seeing their auras, when I touch their skin, I could feel their pain. I literally can even feel their life story. Is that weird?"

"You're preaching to the choir," I laugh.

"More so lately, I look around my room while I'm giving the massage. What do I see out of the corner of my eye? I see what appears to be their dead relatives. It's like they want to deliver a message. Most times I tell them to go away. And they do. But I feel an urgency from them. Like they really want me to pass on some message."

"I see." I ask, "What do you think those messages are all about?"

"I'm not sure, that's why I'm calling you!" We both laugh. "Like I said, I feel like there's some urgency about them, like I have to deliver these messages. I just don't know how."

Intuitively, I ask, "What's the urgency?"

She takes a moment to let the answer come to her. From how she is speaking, I can already tell she's very psychic. She's more psychic than she gives herself credit for—like my own story.

The answer comes to her.

"I'd never thought of it like this before. I think I was meant to be a messenger! I do think that in the back of my mind sometimes... Like I was born to use these abilities to heal and to deliver messages. I feel like there's more to it though. Like I said, I'm not sure how."

I smile.

"Yes," I reply. "That was my sense with you as well. You are definitely meant for more, as are many awakening psychics who come my way."

"Wow," she says as she let that realization sink in. "Here I was thinking I just needed help controlling my gifts."

"You're about to go on an interesting journey. Are you ready to find out more?"

"I hope so!" she laughs.

BORN BEING DIFFERENT

Just about everyone is born with some of intuitive or psychic ability. What I find amusing about those like Jackie is they don't realize just how psychic they really are. Being in denial of our abilities is very common.

Why the denial? There's still a general lack of acceptance from society to even mention the word "psychic". Rather than embracing our psychic side, how do we respond as a result? We suppress our gifts. We deny our premonitions or visions. We don't dare share our gifts for fear of being an outcast. We fear being different. Especially as a child, being different is already hard enough. For children learning about their gifts early, there is great shame often associated. To cope, we go into survival mode and hide.

We'll often ask ourselves, "Am I really psychic?" Put it this way, if you weren't already, would you even be asking that question? Let me reassure you now that if you are reading this book, YES, you are psychic!

Instead of asking the question of if you are psychic or not, what I find even more beneficial to ask is this:

"What if psychic abilities are more like a buried treasure? Like a treasure chest of gold waiting to be revealed?"

From working with novices to experienced practitioners, there is always a buried golden treasure. Like Dorothy in the *Wizard of Oz* embarking on the yellow brick road, it's a matter of taking that first step to find out.

INTRODUCING THE 10 STEP JOURNEY

STEP 1: Learn about the different types of psychic abilities. Identify yours.
- What type of psychic am I?
- Was I born with these gifts?
- Can I have more than one type of psychic ability?

STEP 2: Gain awareness about different types of energies. Pinpoint what is your energy, what is not.
- What's the best way to work with the different types of energies?
- How can I release energy that is not mine?
- How do I replenish my energy so I don't feel so drained?

STEP 3: Learn psychic tools to define your psychic boundaries. Further explore energy in a safe and grounded manner. Avoid taking on other people's energies.
- What is an aura?
- How does my aura relate to psychic boundaries, and how do I protect my aura?
- What do I do if other energies get into my aura?

STEP 4: Learn basic energy tools for managing your energy. Prepare for performing higher levels of energy work.
- What is the nature of working with energy?
- How do I transform or transmute energy?
- What self-healing can I do to further clean out my space of others energies?

STEP 5: Gain more clarity into your specific psychic senses. Experience an introduction to healing your chakras.

- What is a chakra?
- How do I clean out the body-being connection of each chakra?
- How do I connect even more deeply to my specific psychic gifts?

STEP 6: Learn how to "raise your vibration" and how to keep your vibration high.

- What are the practical steps to raising my vibration at a crown chakra level?
- How do I raise my vibration in preparation for giving a reading or healing?
- What are the pitfalls of reading from a lower vibration?

STEP 7: Activate your psychic third eye to perform a basic psychic reading.

- How do I setup to read?
- What do I tune into when reading?
- How do I make separations when I am done with the reading?

STEP 8: Perform a karma-free healing without absorbing other people's energies.

- What are the pitfalls to avoid when giving a healing?
- How do I setup to heal?
- How do I make separations when I am done with the healing?

STEP 9: Learn ways to work with beings, entities, or spirit guides.

- How can I become more senior to beings?
- How do I safely communicate with a being?
- How do I get them to leave?

STEP 10: BONUS ADD-ON: Elevate your energy work psychic manifestation tools.

- How do I create what I want in the 3D world with energy tools?
- What is the true energy behind manifesting?
- How do I work with Spirit to manifest my dreams?

Want more insight into what I've noticed are the 3 Stages to the Psychic Awakening Journey? Check out my mini-masterclass here: MyPsychicAwakening.com/3-stages

Then, continue onto STEP 1 of the process: Learn about the different types of psychic abilities. Identify your gifts.

By Joe Gacoscos

CHAPTER 4 – STEP 1: IDENTIFY YOUR GIFT

P AM COMES IN FOR HER FIRST COACHING SESSION. She identifies with being an highly sensitive empath. As a medical professional, she sees sick patients every day. Her need for coaching stems from her not wanting to not absorb everyone else's energies daily. Here's how her first session unfolds:

"When I first start working with new clients, I like to start off with a 'psychic cat scan' of your space. Would that be okay with you?"

Pam replies, "Of course. Umm, what are you checking for exactly?"

"Great question," I reply. "When I do a psychic cat scan, I take a clairvoyant look at your aura and chakras. This gives me clues into your specific gifts and challenges.

"In case you don't know, chakras are energy centers of the body which we will go more in depth into later.

"When I read clairvoyantly, that means I can see energy. My eyes are closed the whole time. As the reading goes, I'll report to you what I see pops into my mind's eye. How does that sound to you?"

"That sounds great!"

"To begin, when I look at your space, what lights up for me to start, is I see some energy in your belly area. Compared to when I look at your own unique vibration, these energies in your belly appear as dark spots. These clearly aren't yours. This tells me that when you read other people, you tend to empathize with others. You feel what they feel. Another term for this is 'Clairsentience''."

"That's so true," she says, "I do feel everything others around me are feeling..."

"Yes, and I see that there is a build-up of other people's energies. Your 2nd chakra, which is in the belly area, looks full of greys and dark purples to me. What I get from this is because you are processing so many of other people's energies and emotions, I can see how it affects many other areas of your life. These energies look like they leave you feeling sluggish or even overwhelmed. Simply put, it looks like your 2nd chakra is a little blown out, like a deflated tire. On top of that, it appears that there's not much more room for your energy. At all."

"No wonder..." she replies.

"Additionally, I see this blue energy above your head where your crown chakra is located. It looks like you access a lot of information from your crown. Your crown is the 'knowing' space. We call this claircognition. You just know things—beyond intellectual knowing. At the moment, however, it appears that energy is just hanging out above your head, and not quite coming in. Therefore, what I gather is you are having creativity challenges at the moment."

"Wow... I am working on a creative project at work, and I am having a hard time focusing. With all the stress, it's been hard to be creative."

"Yes. Combine that with what I see in your 2nd chakra, it's as if most of your energy is stuck down there. It's not available for the upper chakras."

"That makes total sense," she sighs.

"I'm taking a look at your other chakras for clues. I do see your 6th chakra, which some people call the '3rd eye', is somewhat closed. This is where you can see energy or what we call 'clairvoyance'. With it this closed, I do see that seeing spirits or even auras is not really your thing. However, I do see these darker greens around your 6th chakra. This tells me some energies are keeping your 6th chakra from fully opening. It reminds of how kids are afraid to look under the bed for fear of what they might see."

"That reminds me," she said. "Growing up, I did see what looked like my uncle standing in the corner of my room. He had passed away a few months earlier. I had never met him. When I described what I saw to my mom, she said, 'You just described your Uncle.' It freaked me out and it freaked my mom out. We never spoke about that again."

"Life experience like that is usually when we decide to suppress our abilities," I explain. "This probably explains why seeing energy is not really your main talent for the moment."

I continue with the reading, "I do see bright colors in your imagination space, your mind's eye if you will. And that does appear to be quite active. You can visualize things."

"Yes, when I am super creative, I can see images pop into my mind. I can literally see whole plans all at once, kind of like seeing the big picture. What's interesting is I also see the details of the big picture. It took me awhile to figure out not everyone is like this."

"That's very true," I reply. "That's the challenge of us highly sensitive people is sometimes it is hard for people to relate."

"Oh tell me about it!"

Being highly sensitive, not to mention being very much an empath myself, I smile knowingly.

"The last thing I am going to check for are what are known as your clairauditory channels. This is your ability to hear messages from spirit. This involves your 5th chakra located right at your throat area. The 5th chakra is also involved with telepathy."

"Ah. Interesting."

"With you, I don't necessarily see a lot of beings around your space. Sometimes, I'll literally see a being hanging out on someone's shoulder. The entity is constantly whispering in their ear. With you, I don't see that. Now when it comes to your telepathy, I see a lot of children energy. It's as if you are having to deliver some of your communication telepathically to them. This is in addition to speaking out loud. By chance, do you have kids?"

She laughs. "No. No kids. But I am around kids a lot with my nieces and nephews."

"Haha. No wonder," I laugh.

"In summary, I see you feel a lot, you have the *clairsentience* thing going. You are quite experienced at that. I see with your knowing, or *claircognition*, you do access that space often. With the *clairvoyance*, you don't quite see energy like auras and spirits, but you do see pictures in your mind's eye. From your childhood story, looks like that ability is suppressed. And lastly, with your *clairaudience*, you don't necessarily hear messages from spirit. However, your *telepathic* channels can definitely use a clean-out. With all the kids you are dealing with, this is natural.

"And that's your psychic cat scan."

"Wow. How do you do that?

I smile to Pam. "Stay tuned. Over the course of this program, this is what you learn eventually."

As you review the story above, notice those parts where you resonated with Pam's "psychic cat scan". Take a moment to review your own internal experiences. When it comes to reacting energy, do you

- Feel?
- Know?
- See?
- Hear?
- Experience energy (such as channeling or mediumship)?

Additionally, when you consider how much you favor one sense over the other, are you

- Experienced?
- Novice?
- Somewhere between?
- Unsure?

Take a moment to journal your answers.

THE DIFFERENT TYPES OF ABILITIES

The following are general descriptions for the different types of psychic abilities. For this section I will have you both read the text AND meditate on each ability. <u>It's okay to open then close your eyes as you continue reading through each step</u>. When it comes to figuring out which psychic type you are, just know it's not an exercise of perfection. Rather, it's an act of exercising your own intuition to see what you resonate with the most.

You'll notice I am keeping these descriptions rather light. This is because this is *not* anything for you to analyze or think about too deeply. Rather, as you read the descriptions, see which one you resonate with the most. Feel into it. Check in with your body. Check for strong intuitive "hits". From deep within or even around you, get a *read* on yourself and your abilities.

The fact is, many people have more than one area where they can be equally proficient so it's important to not be too attached to one or the other. No one ability is better than the other either. Your various abilities open up and sharpen over time.

CLAIRCOGNITION
- Associated with the 7th chakra or crown
- Knowingness
- Area of activity
    - On top of the head
    - Area slightly above the head
- Examples:
    - You think of someone, and next thing you know, they're texting you
    - You have an experience of de ja vu, when you enter a new place for the first time
    - You having a knowingness of major world events before they happen (earthquakes, flash floods, or other mass tragedies)

CLAIRVOYANCE
- Associated with the 6th chakra or 3rd eye

- Seeing
- Area of activity
  - Above your brow
  - Middle of forehead
  - Your mind's eye
  - Your place of imagination
  - Center of head (location of the pineal gland)
- Examples:
  - You see auras or spirits
  - You see energy as colors, shapes, images
  - Images form in your mind's eye that you sense aren't just simply your imagination

CLAIRAUDIENCE
- Associated with the 5th chakra
- Hearing and communicating without speaking out loud to Spirit
- Area of activity
  - Throat area
  - Auditory canals
  - Sinuses
- Examples
  - You hear the voices of spirit
  - You get auditory messages from spirit guides or angels
  - You have conversations with dead relatives

TELEPATHY
- Associated with the 5th chakra
- Hearing and communicating without speaking out loud in the physical realm, e.g. to other people or to pets
- Area of activity

- o Throat area
- o Auditory canals
- o Sinuses
- Examples
  - o You hear others thoughts without them saying a word
  - o You send a message or a thought to someone seated next to you
  - o The person somehow reports thinking what you were thinking at the same time

CLAIRSENTIENCE
- Associated with the 2nd chakra
- Feeling and empathizing
- Area of activity
  - o Belly
  - o Where you get a feel for things
  - o Where you follow your gut
- Examples
  - o You not only feel what's going on with others, you feel *why* something is happening
  - o You have a strong sense of empathy
  - o You feel like a sponge for other people's emotions

MEDIUMSHIP/CHANNELING
- Associated with the 7th, 6th & 5th
- You experience energy, i.e. you bring energies into your body to experience it
  - o For example, you might channel an Archangel
  - o You might channel relatives who had passed away to deliver messages

- o You become a different character altogether (very common with actors)
- Area of activity
  - o Energies may come in through your 7th chakra or top of the head
  - o The experience can be a full body experience
  - o Your voice
- Examples
  - o You may say something and then immediately ask yourself, "Was that my voice? Did I just say that?"
  - o You have a fully body experience including voice modulations and body movement
  - o You may speak a foreign language, sing, or speak the light language of intergalactic beings

MEDITATION: THE DIFFERENT TYPES OF ABILITIES

Follow these steps to discover your specific type of psychic ability at an even deeper level. You very well may have more than one. Many report having an ability that is more dominant than the other.

Close your eyes during this exercise. It's okay to open and close your eyes so you can refer back and forth to the text:

Meditation:
(Est. time: 15-20 minutes)
Take a deep breath and settle into your body for a moment.

Start with the first ability listed above, Claircognition. Read through the description of the first ability and examples.

Close your eyes and imagine you can breathe right into the area being described. For example, breathe right into the crown chakra located on top of your head.

Take notice of the activity in that area.
How does it feel?
What do you see?
What energies do you notice?
Don't sense anything? That's fine, too.
Whatever you do, don't force this exercise.
Rather, just allow your own internal wisdom to provide you insights.

Then inquire. Where or when in your life do you find yourself naturally activating or utilizing this area?
Take a brief scan of your life from childhood to present day.
What significant memories come up?
What conversations?
What visions?
What seemingly coincidental moments?

Open your eyes.
Take a moment to journal what came up for you.
Move onto the description of the next ability
Repeat the above steps
Enjoy your insights!

By Joe Gacoscos

STARSEEDS, INDIGOS, CRYSTAL AND RAINBOW CHILDREN

Many times I encounter people who have "All of the Above" when it comes to their psychic abilities. I want to give a special shout out to this special group. This group I will for the sake of brevity, just keep to a single category. I call this group Starseeds. You may have heard about other categories such as Indigos, Crystal, or Rainbow children. They do have their nuances. However, I find they all have similar challenges. Therefore, for this book I will simply refer to them as a single group.

What's unique about Starseeds is their senses seem to be extra heightened. You would think that it would be such a gift to have all these abilities. However, what I find is the opposite is true. With this group of people, they are often struggling, if not suffering.

I know for a fact, many of you reading this can relate.

Why is it so tough for Starseeds? Here's the challenge:

Many Starseeds have already lived multiple lifetimes with these abilities. Many are masters in other realms, galaxies, star systems, or other dimensions. In these other realms of existence, these Starseeds do what we are unable to on the Earthly plane. Examples of this include teleportation, telepathy, bi-location, and telekinesis.

Does this sound a little out there?

Consider this: If you believe in past lives, who's to say all our past lives were only lived on this planet? Who's to say our soul hasn't taken on other forms in these other realms, galaxies, or dimensions? Who's to say these extraordinary abilities, teleportation for example, aren't *normal* in these other realms?

Let's get back to the struggling Starseed. Here's why it is tough for Starseeds here in this Earthly plane. Imagine being able to teleport to anywhere, or speak telepathically. You get your results in an *instant*. However, in our linear, 3D realm of existence, we deal with space and time. What this means is rather than teleport somewhere, we have to drive for hours. Rather than telepath, we actually need to speak to each other. We have to learn to communicate our thoughts and feelings.

Oh what an inconvenience!

In other words, Starseeds often report this dimension as way too slow, too thick, and too suffocating. This is in comparison to where they came from originally. Rather than move more fluidly and seamlessly, there's a HUMAN BODY to contend with. This human body feels extremely limiting to the Starseed. Many Starseeds hate living in their human vessel altogether.

COMMON SIGNS YOU ARE A STARSEED

Here's a list of signs you may be a Starseed:
- All your channels are quite open, especially at a young age
- You're thought of as exceptionally wise "beyond your years"
- Others take time to figure things out. You tend to absorb knowledge. You may be that kid at school who didn't have to study and you still received A's on your exams
- Because you are gifted in this way, you don't relate to the average person
- The average person may not relate to you either, including your friends and family
- Your childhood upbringing may have been a rough one
- At times, you are extremely overwhelmed with energies
- Your behavior may often be associated with being erratic. Your sensitivities might be incorrectly diagnosed. Many are placed on medication

- You grow up feeling like you don't belong in your body, like it's the wrong kind of skin
- You often feel an empty longing as you gaze up at the night sky
- You encounter "light language" whether via channeling, drawing pictures, or through sound
- You are drawn to alchemy, healing, inventing, or advanced forms of energy work
- Unity consciousness, 5D awakening, or ascension of the planet mean something to you
- You feel like you've "been there, done that" when waking up to your psychic gifts
- You feel pulled to and overwhelmed by some greater planetary level mission that you 'must' complete
- You feel a yearning for
  - Global healing
  - Teaching advanced spirituality
  - Saving the environment
  - Opening the hearts and minds of millions
  - Global leadership initiatives in technology or science
  - Leading a mass movement towards unification
- You are compelled to say phrases like, "I feel a strong need to heal the planet." Or, "I have a message the whole world needs to hear."

I know this is a long list. Believe it or not, many who I have encountered indeed do say "Yes" to most of the above.

Can you relate?

(Want further clarification on if you are a Starseed? Watch my Youtube video here: MyPsychicAwakening.com/starseed. Be sure to like, comment and follow in the process!)

If you can relate and you are having a hard time, I want you to know one thing:

You are here for a reason and life indeed IS worth living.

My sense is God (or the Universe or "All that Is") has a funny way of helping you evolve more as a soul. Perhaps you are a master of those skills and abilities in those other realms. What if you have incarnated here on this planet so you can gain even more mastery via a human body? What if it is your karma as a soul to gain mastery in space and time? What if gaining mastery just puts you that much closer to ascended mastery? Not only for your Spirit but an entire planet? For the Universe as a whole?

I can write a whole other book on this topic! As a matter of fact, this is the next book I myself feel a pull to write. This future book helps Starseeds learn to be in their human form. It helps them carry out these planetary soul-driven missions. There is an awakening of consciousness happening on this planet. When viewed that way, it is an exciting time to be part of it. Starseeds are a big part of this.

Can't wait for that future book? Rest assured, continue following the processes laid out in this book. You take those important next steps to overcoming the overwhelm you feel.

Looking for more support as a Starseed now? Check out https://www.facebook.com/groups/MyPsychicAwakening to connect with a community of like-minded souls.

TAKE THE PSYCHIC ABILITIES QUIZ!

By Joe Gacoscos

What's your dominant psychic type(s)? Need more help figuring it out? Check out a fun "2-Minute Psychic Abilities Test". It's not meant to be an end-all, be-all. Taking the quiz helps give you additional insights.

Take the quiz here: MyPsychicAwakening.com/Quiz

Now that you've gained some insight into your abilities, let's take it to the next level, shall we? Continue to STEP 2: Gain awareness of the different type of energies. Pinpoint what is your energy, what is not.

CHAPTER 5 – STEP 2: ENERGY AWARENESS

JOHN IS A LONG-TIME CLIENT who comes in for a deep transformational healing session. He is an active duty member of the Navy. He recently comes back from a six-month deployment out to sea. While out to sea, he lives in cramped quarters with his fellow shipmates 24/7. Learn more about his challenges with his energy:

"I'm so glad to be back," John says. "While on deployment, I felt so drained all the time by these energy vampires. It's like they're sucking the life out of me."

"On top of that, I feel like people can just throw their energies at me. I feel like an energy sponge!" he says. "It's exhausting.

"Being cramped with these energy vampires day in and day out didn't help much either."

I nod. "So if I can paraphrase for a moment, you feel robbed of your own energy from these energy vampires. And on top of that, you feel like you're absorbing everyone else's energy."

"Yes! That's exactly it. I get overwhelmed, confused even. Sometimes I don't even know who I am. I don't know how to feel sometimes. I don't know what to do next."

I assure him, "You know, as a sensitive psychic myself, I can totally relate. It's like you are a car that is supposed to run on super-unleaded gasoline. Instead, you're filled with diesel fuel."

"How would your car run if that's the case?" I ask.

"For sure, the car would break down. And that's exactly how I feel—like I'm running on the wrong kind of fuel."

"Exactly. Fortunately, I have some simple energy tools to help you move other people's energies out. More tools help you bring your energy—the right kind of fuel—back. Are you interested in learning more?"

"Yes, please! I'm ready to go!"

THE POWER OF AMUSEMENT

Before we move onto learning about these powerful energy tools, I want to bring up the energy of Amusement. For those that are extra sensitive to energies, it's hard to navigate all these energies around us. This is where amusement energy comes in to play. Before we dig into amusement, first a quick story:

There I am at around 12 years old, and my mom is leading a group prayer for ten people. Unfortunately, the prayer is for her friend's father who had recently passed away. We're all there, kneeling in front of statues of Jesus, the Virgin Mary, and a picture of the man who just died. It is a solemn scene.

Towards the end of the prayer, my younger sister and I start chuckling about something. I don't remember about what. The chuckle turns into stifled laughter. My mom glares at us like, "This is NOT the time." And so, we try to stop laughing.

Minutes later, we start laughing yet again. We try so hard to hold back. In our brother-sister world, we are in such amusement and play! We can't help laughing. We sound like mini-snorting pigs trying to stifle our laughs! Moments later, I look up to see one of the adults stifling her laugh. She covers her mouth trying not to join in. One of the other kids and another adult also start laughing.

Thank God we get to the final "Amen". At that point, all ten of us including my mom burst out into laughter. In a laughing fit, one of the high school kids states, "I don't even know what's funny! We're praying for someone who just died. This isn't supposed to be funny! But something is!"

Such is the power of amusement. Imagine being in such amusement that you can even laugh at a funeral. Of course, I would advise there are more appropriate times to laugh! Can you remember back to a time where you started laughing for no reason? Or just because someone else was laughing? The reason for the laughs, especially when it seems there's no real reason, is because of the energy of Amusement.

How does this apply to working with your psychic abilities?

Put it this way, how are your psychic experiences when you are *not* in amusement? Scary? Overwhelming?

I tell my students all the time, "The moment you get serious, this psychic stuff doesn't work."

Here's the great thing about being in amusement. When you really start to apply it, it does not matter what energies you encounter. Being in amusement is the ultimate antidote. As you continue this journey, if you learn nothing else, be in amusement.

If you feel like this isn't working, be in amusement about it feeling like it's not working. If you aren't able to get yourself in amusement, be in amusement about not being amused!

Find multiple ways to get yourself in amusement. Watch a funny video. Smile. Laugh often.

How amused are you right now? Pretty amused? Can you *choose* to be more amused?

Like a child, what if reading the rest of this book is like playing a game? How amused can you be right now?

P.S. Did I mention how important it is to be in amusement for psychic work?

P.P.S. Amusement. I think you get the point ;-)

NOT MY ENERGY

At the beginning of this chapter, client John brings up his story about feeling drained of his energy while at the same time, feeling like he's filled with everyone else's energies. This is true especially if you are empathic, clairsentient, or highly sensitive in general.

What John brings up are two important questions:
- What is your energy?
- What is *not* your energy?

First, let's start with 'what is *not* your energy'. The reason to start here is because we are so filled with other people's energies so often. We begin to believe how it is *is* how we are. Said another way, you get so used to other people's energies in your space. You begin to believe that energy *is* your energy.

Does that make sense?

Before moving on, check in with yourself. Sense where you resonate with that last paragraph.

You might say to yourself, "Oh yeah! That's not my energy. That's my mom's energy." Or, "For sure, that's not my energy.

That's energy I brought home from work." When you get to this point, you start to expand your awareness.

You start to differentiate vibrationally.

When you tap into what's *not* yours, then you can start to tap into what is *your* energy.

The following meditation helps to distinguish what is and what isn't your energy:

MEDITATION FOR MY ENERGY, NOT MY ENERGY

Follow these steps to discover what is your energy, what is not. The more you practice differentiating, the better reader you become. Building this muscle to read your energy sets you up nicely for the future chapters.

Meditation:
(Est. time: 10-15 minutes)
Take a nice deep breathe, close your eyes, and bring in some amusement energy. It's okay to open and close your eyes so you can refer back and forth to the text.

Take an intuitive scan of your space:
Your body.
Your energy field or your aura.
Anywhere you might have an ache, pains, headache, or any feeling of stuckness are good places to start.
Any energy that is not your energy you may sense as dark spots, a static grey to white; they may feel heavy to you.

When you encounter these energies, ask yourself, "Is that my energy? Or is that not my energy?" Take a moment. See what intuitive response you get.

Find another spot, or even a memory that might come up. Ask yourself again, "Is that my energy? Or is that not my energy?"

Continue to other spots, memories, or other energies you are sensing. Get a sense of the unique vibration each energy has.
Is it heavy or darker?
Or is it lighter?

Take a nice deep breath and you can come out of the trance. Make note of what you noticed.

Journal your experience or observations.

Would prefer guided meditations instead? You can access many of the meditations in the "Awaken Your Psychic Gifts in 7 Days Mini-Challenge". Follow along as I guide you, or you can choose to do the meditation on your own.

Here's how to interpret what you encountered:
- Normally our own energies are a bright pastel color—bright blue, bright green or a bright purple, for example

- Anything that is *not* your energy usually shows up as darker or it vibrates slower
- As in client John's story at the beginning of this chapter, what distinguish what kind of "fuel" are you mostly running on. Other people's energies? Or your own?
- If mostly not your own energy, can you sense how you might be feeling run down?

Congrats! You now have distinguished what's yours and not your energy. Let's move onto tools you can use to move other people's energies out, and bring back your own energy to replenish you.

GROUNDING AND GOLDEN SUN

Imagine for a moment sink full of dirty water going down the drain. Gravity takes hold. The sink releases all that dirty water.

Your body is like that sink. Your body holds all kinds of energies that can make your space like "dirty water". When you "ground", this helps you to drain away these energies that are not yours. In the next meditation you will learn about a "grounding cord". This grounding cord acts like the drain of a sink, helping you drain away these excess energies.

Additionally, the grounding cord provides the foundation for more advance energy work. Like trees rooted to the ground, or like an anchor of a ship, the grounding cord helps the body feel safe and secure. This especially necessary for working with different kinds of energies in future chapters.

When your space is clear, this is where you can next replenish. Like emptying out a closet full of old clothes, you can now fill it in with whatever you want. Why not fill it in with your own energy instead?

This is where we use a "golden sun" energy tool. Like the sun in the middle of our solar system, this sun has a powerful gravitational force. Imagine a golden sun in your mind's eye. Via your imagination alone, the golden sun brings back your energy from wherever you may have left it. It's like gathering all the pieces of you you might have left behind journeying through life.

WHY USE GOLD?

Before getting to the meditation, I want to make a special remark about gold. Gold is a very high, spiritual vibration. You will notice many spiritual traditions, religions, and cultures are surrounded by gold. Even the metal gold is one of the most precious metals on this planet.

This is why we work with this energy. When you bring back all your energy into this golden sun as described above, you raise your energy to gold. Imagine how all that golden goodness feels when that energy infuses into your body. You feel replenished with your own life force energy.

You replace all the *not yours* energy you released by grounding. Since it is your imagination of gold, you then replenish with your own energy. It's an energizing experience.

Ready to try grounding and replenishing with a golden sun?

MEDITATION: GROUNDING AND GOLDEN SUN

Follow these steps to help you let go and replenish energies from your space. Building on top of what is your energy, what is not, create a "grounding cord" to help you release any energy that is not yours. Create a golden sun to bring back your energy for replenishment.

The steps are listed below. Rather listen to my voice as I guide you through these meditations instead? Check out the sampler video taken straight from my "Awaken Your Psychic Gifts in 7 Days Challenge". Follow along with my voice as well as get even more insider information not found in this book:

By Joe Gacoscos

Meditation:
(Est. time: 10-15 minutes)
Be seated upright, close your eyes, and with lots of amusement, take a nice deep breath. It's okay to open and close your eyes so you can refer back and forth to the text.

Take an intuitive scan of your space. Where do you see, sense, or feel any energies in your space that are not yours?

At the base of your spine, imagine a healing green ball of energy forming as wide as your hips. Imagine gravity taking hold of this green ball, sending it down to the center of the planet, leaving behind a solid green tube of energy.

This is your "grounding cord".

Like the trees solidly rooted to the earth, or like an anchor of a ship firmly planted at the seabed, imagine your body being solidly connected to the center of Mother Earth.

With lots of amusement and play, imagine the energy that's not yours start draining away and releasing out of your body, like dirty water draining down a sink.

Notice how that feels to the body as you release and let go of all the energy that's not yours.

Witness or feel as that energy reaches the center of the planet, imagining that energy turn back to pure energy for Mother Earth to recycle.

Once you have made enough room in your space, your body, and your aura, now imagine a large golden sun start to form about 3 feet above your head.

Playfully imagine the powerful gravitational pull of this golden sun bringing back all your energy from wherever it's been left behind
~ From other people
~ Work
~ Projects
~ Conversations
~ Clients
~ Family
~ Friends
~ The past
~ And even past lives

As you watch your energy return, the golden sun gets larger and fuller.

When the golden sun is nice and full, invite that golden energy to come in through the top of your head, the crown chakra.

Like pouring water into a glass, imagine all the golden light of your energy pouring into you, filling up every single cell of your body, and especially any empty spaces from grounding.

Fill in your energy field in front of you, behind you, to the sides, above and below you.

Have it be that you are like a glowing, golden lightbulb of your own energy.

When you are completely filled up, lean over to release any excess energy.

Take a deep breath, stretch out your body a bit, and come out of the trance.

Journal your experiences.

How was that to let go of energies that aren't yours?

How was that to then to replenish with your energy?

When students experience this the first time, they report feeling renewed and reinvigorated. They feel lighter, like a weight has been lifted.

You now you have a better experience of what is and is not your energy. You know how to release and replenish your energy with grounding and golden suns. It's now time to explore what exactly is "your space".

Read on for STEP 3: Learn psychic tools to define your psychic boundaries and basic tools for psychic protection.

CHAPTER 6 INTRO

CHAPTER 6 – STEP 3: PSYCHIC BOUNDARIES & PROTECTION

A CLIENT NAMED JANINE COMES IN FOR A COACHING SESSION. She is into week 3 of working with the tools of grounding and replenishing with a golden sun. Janine is already a professional psychic. She has no formal training, however. She especially wants to learn better psychic protection and about establishing her boundaries. She is your typical wide-open psychic before coming to see me.

"Something happened to me when I started doing tarot cards years ago," says Janine. "I swear it opened up some door, or some portal."

"Tell me more about that," I respond.

"It's not necessarily when I'm doing readings for other people. It's more when I'm not reading that's the problem."

"Interesting," I say.

"It started off innocently enough," she says. "The more I read, the better the readings became. People started asking me to do readings. I figured I was just a natural. However, as time passed, I started getting, you know, visitors from the other side."

"I see...How's your experience been with that lately?"

"I'm not afraid of them or anything, thank goodness. I figure they're just spirits like the rest of us."

She continues, "However, I live near a hospital. And you know, there's a lot of people that die in hospitals. I think I get visitors from that hospital almost every night. This never happened before, not till I started really getting into tarot."

"In all honesty, I'm more annoyed than anything. They come at the weirdest and most random times."

I laugh. I then ask, "How do they present themselves?"

"I don't really see energy like you do. But I do know they're there. I just know. And sometimes, I get this really irritating ringing in my ears. And I know I'm not sick. I don't have any ear infections or anything like that."

"Yes, I used to get that ringing a lot, too," I say. "Spirits often vibrate at a higher frequency than we do with the physical body. So, when they're communicating with you, you'll often experience that higher kind of frequency. You experience the high-pitched ringing in the ears. In the Clairvoyant programs, we tell these spirits to lower their vibration a bit. This is so we can communicate with them more easily."

Fascinated, she replies, "That explains why that ringing seems so intense."

I continue, "Overall, it sounds to me like you are ready to learn about psychic boundaries. These psychic protection tools help so these beings don't just come in whenever they want. Would that be of interest to you?"

Relieved, she says, "That would be great."

YOUR PSYCHIC SPACE: THE AURA

In the previous chapter, you learn to ground energies out of your space. You replenish your energy in with golden suns. There's much freedom that comes from releasing those energies. You give yourself more room for your energy.

At this point, however, you might be wondering, "Joe, what exactly do you mean by 'your space?'"

Imagine for a moment a large rock sitting in the heat of a desert sun. As the day goes, the rock absorbs the heat from the sun. You walk by this rock and put your hand near it. You feel the heat coming off the rock. You move your hand away a bit, and you feel heat from the surroundings. You move your hand closer and closer to the rock. Once again, you feel the heat more specifically coming off of the rock. In essence, it is like you are feeling the energy field—or the aura—of the rock.

Now imagine stepping away from the desert to standing in line at a grocery store. Imagine while standing there, someone stands really close behind you. You don't even have to turn around. You *know* or you can *feel* that person standing behind you. "Annoying," you think to yourself, "get out of my personal space!" You move so that person isn't in your aura or your energy field.

As with feeling heat from the hot desert rock, you can also feel the aura of the person standing behind you. With the person at the grocery store, they are literally a) walking into your aura, and b) their energy is getting into yours.

What's fascinating about the aura is it is just like the desert rock. The rock absorbs heat from the sun. Likewise, your aura absorbs all kinds of energies—other people's energies, emotions and thoughts. Being the sensitive psychics we are, we can often sense those energies in our own auras. We sense energies in other people's auras quite strongly as well. This is why when you walk by a total stranger, you might say to yourself, "Wow, I can feel his negative energy."

Quick story about my experience with auras in my former corporate day job:

My boss calls me into his office. He yells at me about something. I forget exactly about what. What I do remember is he yells...more like he lets off steam *at* me. In that moment, I can *feel* him throwing his energy at me as his energy lands in my aura. I start to coil away.

This is how my former boss operates; to throw energy as a form of control and dominance. Subconsciously, he knows this makes people feel like they're lesser-than.

As we learned in the last chapter, when it's not your energy, it just plain doesn't feel good in your space. The point of this former boss story is the aura feels just as real as the physical body. This is especially true when you bring your awareness to how it feels when it gets filled with foreign energies.

The good news is by bringing awareness to your spiritual anatomy, you can then do something about it. Not only can you protect your space, you know exactly what to protect! We'll get to that in just a moment. First, let's get to know the aura.

MEDITATION: FINDING THE EDGE OF YOUR AURA

For this meditation, you get familiar with your aura. Furthermore, you will define the edge of your aura. This edge is your psychic boundary. Anything within this boundary is YOUR UNIVERSE. Anything outside of your aura is THE REST OF THE UNIVERSE. You have enough on your plate, right? Let's start by focusing on your own aura, i.e. your Universe, and all that's within your Universe.

(Would you rather listen to this and the other meditations found in this book? These meditations are found in the "Awaken Your Psychic Gifts in 7 Days Mini Challenge".)

Meditation:
(Est. time: 15-20 minutes)
Close your eyes, breathe, and with a sense of amusement, give yourself a fresh grounding cord. It's okay to open and close your eyes so you can refer back and forth to the text.

Imagine, feel, or sense your aura, your own energy field.

You might sense it like a bubble around you. Or an orb. Or it might be egg shaped.

Silently ask yourself, "Where is the edge of my aura?"
What do you sense?
Is the edge two feet away? Three feet? Five feet?
For a male body, the edge is typically 2 feet away from the body.
For a female body, usually the edge is typically 3 feet away. This is because the female body typically runs more creative energy (i.e. think creating life within the womb).
When in stress, the aura can either deflate, around 6 inches away or it can be spread out 5 to 10 feet!
Some big personalities literally "fill up a room" with their auras.

Through either visualization or simply intention (or both), bring your aura to about 2 feet away from you.

Rub your hands together to wake up your hand chakras so you can more easily feel energy with your hands.
Find the edge of your aura with your hands:
With your palms facing away from you, slowly push your hands in front of you till you feel the edge of your aura.
When you reach out as far as you can go, you can face your palms towards you and start pulling your hands back.

Sense any signs, even if you think it might just be your imagination:
You might feel a buzzing in your hands.
Your hands might feel a tingling.
You might feel you are bumping up against something, like the edge of a soft pillow.

With your hands still out, open your eyes. See if where your hands are match where you imagined the edge of your aura to be two feet away.
This is your psychic boundary.

Bring the edge of your aura to a distance that feels most comfortable to you.

Fill yourself—your body and your aura—in with a golden sun. Notice how that feels to the body.

Take a deep breath, stretch and come out of the meditation.

BONUS: Ask a friend to sit down in front of you. Have her stretch the edge of her aura out to three feet. Repeat the above steps to find the edge of your friend's aura with your hand chakras. Have your friend tell you if you are close or not. Have fun trying this out a few times with different people and different distances.

As before, lots of amusement! Play with this.

Journal your experiences.

MEDITATION: PSYCHIC PROTECTION ROSE

In this meditation, you learn a tool I teach my students in the Clairvoyant training programs. In addition to the grounding cord and golden sun, I now introduce to you a Rose.

A rose has a lot of energy to it. Many ancient religions and traditions often refer to roses. You can certainly try using any other symbol other than a rose. I prefer roses as that's how I'm trained. I find the more consistent you are with whatever tools you use, the more powerful the tool becomes over time.

Meditation:
(Est. time: 5-10 minutes)
Close your eyes, breathe, and with a sense of amusement, give yourself a fresh grounding cord. It's okay to open and close your eyes so you can refer back and forth to the text.

Give a silent "hello" to the edge of your aura as discovered in the previous meditation.

Now imagine a rose sitting right on the edge of your aura. Imagine it like a rose sitting on top of a soft pillow.

With the rose sitting at the edge of your aura, get the sense of it further defining your boundaries. There's your side of the rose, and there's the other side of the rose.

Now imagine this rose is a magnet for other energies that are not yours.
If someone throws energy at you, it goes into the rose rather than your aura.

Now imagine the rose being very capable. If energy comes from behind you, imagine the rose just sliding behind you to catch that energy.
If any energy happens to sneak into your aura, imagine the rose vacuuming all that energy out.
With your protection rose in front of you, fill yourself in with a golden sun.

BONUS: Imagine playing out a scene from your past where you had a heated conversation with someone. Play that scene out in your mind's eye.
Now, hit "rewind". This time, imagine you have a protection rose in front you, catching all of that other person's energy. How does that scene play out now?

Journal your experiences.

THE NEUTRAL SEAT OF THE SOUL

There is one more "space" for you to establish your psychic boundaries and lay claim to. This space is the center of your head.

By Joe Gacoscos

Right in the center of your head is where your pineal gland is located. This is located between the hemispheres of your brain, and right between the front and back of your head. It's said that the pineal gland is the Spiritual gland of the body. Bring your awareness to this space. You can then more easily access higher spiritual energies.

The center of your head is also known as the "neutral seat of the soul". By bringing all your awareness into this center, you experience energy from a more neutral vantage point. Imagine when you are *not* neutral to energies. It is much easier to get swept away and overwhelmed when you are not neutral.

As you go through the following meditation, there is an important distinction. You should find the experience of being in the center of your head is different from simply "being in your head." You may have heard people say, "Get out of your head." That space is not what I'm referring to.

The former, being in the center, is about neutrality. Imagine it as being in your central command center for the body. You might imagine the old Star Trek shows with the captain of the ship seated in the control bridge. He commands the ship and sees all from the big monitor in front of him.

On the other hand, the latter of "being in your head", has no focus. You go wherever your mind wanders. Your awareness may not actually be in your head at all! Your point of awareness may even be outside of your body.

Said another way, being in the center of your head means you actually are in your body. Your awareness can expand out to the edge of the Universe if you want it to. What if you were to concentrate your focus your awareness to a single point instead?

For this purpose, choose being right in the center of the head as a single platform for your awareness.

In the meditation that follows, you experience the feel of this for yourself.

MEDITATION: ACCESSING THE NEUTRAL SEAT OF THE SOUL

For this meditation, you will be led to finding the center of your head. Once you locate the center, you bring all your energy and attention to that point. From there, you can imagine this place, this neutral seat of the soul as being like your command center. It's like you are in the control center of your own ship.

Meditation:
(Est. time: 15-20 minutes)
Close your eyes, breathe, and with a sense of amusement, give yourself a fresh grounding cord. It's okay to open and close your eyes so you can refer back and forth to the text.

Find where your attention is at now.
Is it outside of your body?
Is it in your belly? In your heart? Somewhere where there's pain in your body?
Is some of your energy still at work? With your last conversation?

Imagine where your center of your head is.
The best way I have found is simply to silently ask the question, "Where is the center of my head located?"
Your body, your consciousness, and your inner wisdom simply give you the answer.

By Joe Gacoscos

Alternatively, imagine the following:
A line that stretches from the top of your ear to the opposite ear.
Another line from between your brow to the back of your head.
And another line right at the center of the top of your head extending downward.
Where all those lines intersect is the center of your head.

Find wherever your energy and attention is now. Imagine all your energy sliding right into the space right in the center of head.

From now on, you can claim this as your neutral place from which to work with energy.

Imagine a mini-grounding cord from this center of head extending down to your main grounding cord.
With lots of amusement, imagine any foreign energy sliding down into the main grounding cord.
Notice the clarity you gain from clearing the center of your head.

What's it is like to experience, see, or sense the world from this vantage point?

From the center of head, imagine a big gold sun above your head and fill yourself in. Take a moment to look around, both with your eyes closed, then with your eyes open.

Take a deep breath, stretch and come out of trance.

Journal about your experience.

After going through these exercises, many students report feeling a renewed sense of ownership of their space. There's a sense of boundaries that hadn't been defined before.

For the sensitive psychic, this is HUGE. As you learn to define your boundaries more and more, people, beings, and other energies won't affect you as much. This is especially true when you continue practicing being in the center of your head. You can navigate both the physical and spirit realms more easily. We work with spirit in a later chapter. This is a key skill.

The question next comes up, however, "what if energy *does* get in my space? What do I do about that?"

Flip to STEP 4: Learn basic energy tools for managing your energy. Prepare for performing higher levels of energy work.

By Joe Gacoscos

CHAPTER 7 – STEP 4: ENERGY CLEARING

THERE ARE MANY NATURAL HEALERS IN THE WORLD TODAY. You may be a professional healer like Bonnie in the following story. You may be in a healing profession such as nursing, a chiropractor or even a coach. Or, you may simply the extremely caring best friend who never wants to see friends in pain. If you are highly-sensitive, it is highly likely you are a healer at heart as well.

Many healers especially enjoy learning psychic boundaries we learn about in the last chapter. As you learn with Bonnie, healers have an extra challenge clearing out foreign energies.

Find out how Bonnie learns to go beyond psychic boundaries to keeping her energy space clear:

"When I do reiki on my clients, I love the flow of energy," says client Bonnie. "I do a lot of hands-on-healing. I add some massage as well. My clients always feel a shift."

"The problem is," she continues, "I work with around five patients per day. By the end of the day, while my patients feel great, I often feel wiped!"

"And you are grounding, putting your protection rose up?" I ask.

"Yes. I'm using the tools. However, I still feel a need to *clean out* my space. Especially with hands-on healing, it's hard not to take on other people's energies."

"Yes. Of course. I do know what you mean. I love to do readings and healings for others. However, sometimes my body can only take so much. It's at that point, it's time to take care of the body with a good 'clean out'.

"As a matter of fact," I continue, "it's important to not wait till you're feeling like crap before taking care of yourself! All of us should be mindful to clean out often. In your case, I advise cleaning out after each client."

"That would be great! I love what I do. But if I'm to do this as my long-term profession, I can sure stand to clean out more regularly."

"Great! Let's get into managing your energy with self-care and clean outs."

CLUES YOU NEED AN ENERGY CLEAN OUT

For this chapter, you learn tools to clean out your aura, your body, your chakras—i.e. your space. The question becomes, "How often should I clean out? When?"

As mentioned in Bonnie's story, you don't want to wait till you are feeling bad. Nor do you want to get so full of others energies you that you forget who you even are. Here are some tips for when to clean out:

- Whenever you complete client sessions; after every client is ideal
- The end of a long day at work
- After tough conversations
- Whenever you feel overwhelmed with *not yours* energies

Continuing on *without* a clean out from time to time leaves you worn out. Eventually, you get burned out which you can easily avoid.

Personally, I find myself using the following tools sometimes hourly. The more you consciously clean out, the better you manage your energy.

Continue reading to learn how to use "clean out roses" in the following sections.

TRANSFORMING ENERGY

Before we continue to learning about clean outs, you might be wondering, "Joe, what exactly is your definition of healing?"

An important aspect of healing is transforming energy. Often when I work with clients who need healing work, they have some kind of stuck energy in their space. A quick client story:

Charlene, a long-time of mine client texts me one morning, complaining of severe abdominal pain. It's like a psychic 911 emergency call. She texts, "It's so painful, I feel like I'm going to pass out."

I take a quick clairvoyant look. I see these three dark purple spots in her left side. These purple spots look like three stones in a row, right at the bottom of her rib cage. I text her back to tell her what I see. I ask, "Would you like a healing on that?" She texts back, "OMG, Yes!"

Since she is at a distance, I give a "hello" to her as a spirit to start. I then take a "clean out rose", and I imagine using that rose like a feather duster collects up dust. Literally I see this clean-out rose lift the energy up out of her abdomen, and outside of her aura.

I then take that rose and I explode it and everything else contained within the rose. I see that rose literally turn into millions of pieces, as if turning to dust. I fill that spot in with a golden sun to replenish where those stones used to be.

In essence, in my mind's eye, I take what appears in one form, i.e. the clean-out rose filled with that energy. I then explode it to turn it into dust, which in essence *transforms* that energy into another form. Exploding that picture takes the locked charge out of that stuck energy.

Within minutes, Charlene texts me back, "What did you do? Whatever you did, I totally felt that! Seriously, Joe. I was doubled over in pain. You totally helped me. Thank you sooo much!"

In a future chapter, we will cover how to give someone a basic healing. For now, you'll learn how to give yourself a healing so you can manage your own energy.

MEDITATION: MANAGING YOUR ENERGY WITH A CLEAN-OUT ROSE

In this meditation, you learn about how to give yourself a healing with a clean-out rose. Many feel a perceptible shift when exploding and transforming the rose. Does it really work? The following meditation helps you find out:

By Joe Gacoscos

(Would you rather listen to this and the other meditations found in this book? These meditations are found in the "Awaken Your Psychic Gifts in 7 Days Mini Challenge".)

Meditation:
(Est. time: 15-20 minutes)
Close your eyes, breathe, be in the center of your head, and with a sense of amusement, give yourself a fresh grounding cord. It's okay to open and close your eyes so you can refer back and forth to the text.

Scan your aura or your body for any stuck energy. Scan for any energy that is not in present time (i.e. it originates from some incident in the past).

Pinpoint where in your body that energy is located.
How does it feel?
How does it appear?
Whose energy is it?
How is it affecting your energy levels?

Create a fresh rose out in front of you.
Imagine that this is a "clean-out rose".
It can either be sticky like honey to gather up energy.
Or it can be like a vacuum. Let your imagination soar with this one.

With your psychic hands, take that clean-out rose. Use it to collect the stuck energy in your space. See or sense that energy being picked up out of your space. Move this rose outside of your aura, leaving behind an empty space.

With LOTS of amusement, imagine that you can explode that rose into millions of pieces in front of you. What once was a rose turns to dust.

Watch that dust go down your grounding cord to the center of the planet for Mother Earth to recycle.
Fill in the empty space with a mini-golden sun.
Fill in your whole body with a golden sun.

Notice how the body reacts to the transforming of the energy.
You might yawn as your body reacts to the release of energy.
You might feel a void of energy from where heavy energy used to be stuck.
You might feel the golden sun replenishing and reinvigorating your body and aura.
Validate (i.e. acknowledge it is real) this experience for yourself.

Take a deep breath, stretch and come out of trance.

Journal about your experience.

ISN'T IT JUST MY IMAGINATION?

By this point, many of the more inquisitive students are left wondering.

Student Paul inquires. "Joe. This is all well and good. I DO feel something when doing this work. However, isn't this all a product of our imagination?"

I love this question.

I reply, "Isn't our imagination energy, anyway? Furthermore, it's scientifically proven that when we can imagine something, then it tends to manifest with more certainty; world class athletes imagine winning all the time."

Student lightbulbs flash by this point.

"So when it comes to healing," I continue, "YES, it totally IS our imagination. However, our imagination is energy. And since you're using your imagination—and intent—to transform energy, it gets reflected in the physical.

"So let me ask you, did you feel a something shift when you imagined exploding that rose?"

"Yes!" Paul states emphatically.

"And even if it shifts, say only one percent, it's still a healing, is it not?" I ask. "Where you were before has shifted to some place new?"

"Oh absolutely."

"It gives a whole new meaning to healing, doesn't it?"

"I agree."

Many times, I find that when there is a stuck energy, it manifests physically, e.g. a stuck energy in your head manifests as a headache. In this regard, a simple ache shows there is a connection between the spiritual and the physical worlds.

In the next chapter, we dive deeper into what I call the "Body-Spirit Connection". Imagine this connection as a BRIDGE between the physical and spiritual worlds. These connections are found via the seven chakras of the body. We explore and clean out each chakra. In so doing, you enhance your natural psychic abilities to access higher spiritual realms.

The healing continues onto STEP 5: Gain more clarity into your specific psychic senses. Experience an introduction to healing your chakras.

By Joe Gacoscos

CHAPTER 8 – STEP 5: CHAKRAS—BRIDGING BODY AND SPIRIT

CONGRATULATIONS ON MAKING IT TO UP TO THIS POINT! This particular chapter is symbolic in many regards. This is the middle chapter of this book. In previous chapters you learned about your space and your energy. In the following chapters we cover more advanced topics. In essence, this chapter is like a bridge in the middle, taking you from one world and into another.

As it so happens, being a *bridge* is also how I relate to chakras—the bridge between body and spirit.

Now before we get into the topic, I'd like to take a break from the usual pattern thus far. Normally, I begin each chapter telling some cool client story to help you relate to the topic. This time, however, I'd like to check in with you instead!

Thus far you've learned about:

- Identifying your psychic abilities
- Different types of energies
  - Amusement
  - Your energy/not your energy
  - Grounding
  - Golden suns

- Psychic boundaries
    - Your aura
    - Psychic protection
- Managing your energy
    - Transforming energy and exploding roses
    - A new definition of healing

How's it going so far? Have questions? If you haven't already, be sure sign up for your "Awaken Your Psychic Gifts in 7 Days Mini Challenge" to help you along your journey through the rest of this book. Once you sign up, you will also be guided to a secret Facebook™ group for book members only. Post your questions in there. Either I or someone in our light warrior community will reply with an answer within hours.

MEDITATION: CHECK IN WITH YOUR ENERGY

With the above topics in mind, here are a few questions for you to consider. As you read through the following questions, allow yourself to go beyond the mind-chatter. Rather, you can really relax, close your eyes, and sink into your body for a moment. Many who fully engage the questions in this way report being surprised by the answers:

Meditation:
(Est. time: 10-15 minutes)
Close your eyes, breathe, be in the center of your head, and with a sense of amusement, give yourself a fresh grounding cord. It's okay to open and close your eyes so you can refer back and forth to the text.

Ask yourself:
What has shifted in my world thus far?
How was my energy before reading this book?
How is my energy now?
What energies have I released?
What energies am I aware of now where I wasn't before?
What insights and a-ha's have I gained?
What new questions are coming up?

Take a moment to journal your answers. As you journey through the rest of the book, you discover even more facets of yourself. For now, let's hop onto the "Chakra Bridge"!

INTRO TO THE BRIDGE

There is a ton of information on chakras already on the Internet. However, what you will find is not many of those sources relate to chakras as a bridge between the body and spirit as I teach it. Furthermore, much of those texts don't really talk about chakras in the context of psychic development. In the meditations later in this chapter, you explore this very important distinction.

For this chapter, I'll only give a brief overview of each chakra. I can give you a more traditional definition of what each chakra means. I can describe their function. However, what's even more important is what YOU DISCOVER for yourself as you dive deep into each chakra. You gain an even deeper appreciation this way from your own innate wisdom.

I teach a course online multiple times per year called "Ascending the 12 Chakras". What you learn about chakras in this course are that there are seven chakras of the body. There are also five chakras in the transcendent realm outside of the body. Depending on different traditions, you will find there are even more chakras. We will only cover the main seven chakras in this book.

Picture these seven chakras as energy centers. When looked at clairvoyantly, I see them as mini-balls of energy. Some people see them as mini-tornado shaped vortexes. Others see them as camera lenses. There is no right or wrong to this. How you see the chakras or relate to them is your Truth.

In the chakras course, we cover cleaning out each chakra using the methods you have learned about thus far. Gather energy into a rose. Explode the rose. Transform those stuck energies resulting in a healing.

What I find fascinating at the end of each class is invariably, students proclaim, "Oh my gosh. Clearing out my chakras has made a huge difference. My senses are so much clearer now. I feel like I can sense/feel/see energies even more now."

Mind you, this Chakra Awakening course is not meant to be a "How-to-be-More-Psychic" kind of a training. **However, what ends up happening is because of the weekly clean outs of each chakra, each and every student reports feeling more clear. This translates to their senses feeling more intuitive or more psychic!**

As the instructor, I learn that it's less about trying to get students to be more psychic. It's more about cleaning and clearing out stuck energies. You thus uncover your natural psychic abilities waiting to be revealed—like a buried treasure. It's funny how that works.

WORKING SMARTER NOT HARDER

To illustrate this further, imagine a dirty window for a moment. It's dusty. Perhaps you see some caked-on grime on it. Through this dirty window, you can see light shining through. There appears to be a large tree outside, or at least a silhouette of one. You strain your eyes. "Is that really a tree?"

"Oh this is ridiculous," you say to yourself. You spray some window cleaner on. Bust up the dirt. Wipe it clean. Light pours in. It indeed is a tree!

Now imagine, rather than wiping the window, you instead strain your eyes. You strain your eyes even harder, trying to make out if it's really a tree standing out there. "Why strain your eyes" you might ask, "when you can just wipe the dirt away?"

Makes perfect sense, right?

This is what happens with many people first learning to control their psychic senses. They strain. They put lots of effort. In the act of working so hard, they report, "Joe, I don't see anything. This psychic stuff isn't working."

Rather than trying so hard, what if you were simply take a rose and clear out your field of view instead? In this case, for this chapter, this is what we will do for each chakra:

Key take-away: Each chakra is that window between spirit and the body. When we clear the "dirt" off each chakra, in effect we're clearing the spirit-body window. And when we clear off this window, we therefore open up our psychic senses even more!

MEDITATION: CHAKRA DISCOVERY

As mentioned before, I will only give you enough detail on each chakra. What I find is the more details I give to students, the "dirtier the window gets". What's more important is to have each chakra be *clear* instead, not muddied by someone else's definitions.

Here's a brief summary of each chakra. As you read through the descriptions, take a pause to meditate on the energy of each chakra as described. You gain a much deeper understanding of your chakras and yourself with this approach. You may end up spending up to an hour on this meditation which is fine. As always, approach this with the energy of amusement and lots of curiosity:

(Would you rather listen to guided chakra meditations? Chakra Awakening Course is available for in-depth training)

Meditation:
(Est. time: 5 minutes per chakra)
Close your eyes, breathe, be in the center of your head, and with a sense of amusement, give yourself a fresh grounding cord. It's okay to open and close your eyes so you can refer back and forth to the text.
Meditate on each of the following by giving a psychic "hello" to each chakra:

1ST CHAKRA
Location: Base of the spine
Function: Survival, connection to the planet
Challenges: Fear, survival issues around money, loss of connection to community or to the world

Bring your attention to this chakra, meditate, notice what comes up (memories, old energies, old feelings, personal challenges), journal your observations.

2ND CHAKRA

Location: Beneath the belly button

Function: Feeling, processing emotions, sexual energies and relationships

Challenges: Emotional overwhelm, feeling others emotions too much, overactive empath

Bring your attention to this chakra, meditate, notice what comes up (memories, old energies, old feelings, personal challenges), journal your observations.

3RD CHAKRA

Location: Sternum, right where your rib cages meet, below your chest

Function: The "doing" chakra, control, personal power

Challenges: Control or be controlled, spiritual competition, physical identity issues

Bring your attention to this chakra, meditate, notice what comes up (memories, old energies, old feelings, personal challenges), journal your observations.

4TH CHAKRA

Location: Heart, center of chest

Function: Love, self-affinity, compassion

Challenges: Grief, "love is a roller coaster", giving too much of your energy away, heartache

Bring your attention to this chakra, meditate, notice what comes up (memories, old energies, old feelings, personal challenges), journal your observations.

5TH CHAKRA

Location: Throat

Function: Voice, expression, communication

Challenges: Expressing Truth, communicating identity, speaking up for yourself, speaking someone else's truth and not yours

Bring your attention to this chakra, meditate, notice what comes up (memories, old energies, old feelings, personal challenges), journal your observations.

6TH CHAKRA

Location: Center of forehead, above brow

Function: "3rd eye", seeing, intuition, imagination, the mind

Challenges: Illusions and delusions, over-thinking, over-analyzing

Bring your attention to this chakra, meditate, notice what comes up (memories, old energies, old feelings, personal challenges), journal your observations.

7TH CHAKRA

Location: Top of head

Function: Knowingness, opening to world of spirt

Challenges: Too connected with spirit realms, disconnected from own Truth, blurred lines between realities

Bring your attention to this chakra, meditate, notice what comes up (memories, old energies, old feelings, personal challenges), journal your observations.

MEDITATION: DEEP SELF-REFLECTION

With the introduction to each of your chakras, you gain awareness on the location, the function, and the challenges. Before we continue, take a moment to review your journal from the previous exercise. Explore using the following questions:

Is there a theme to your own personal challenges?
What are you surprised about from meditating on each chakra?
What different energy levels do you sense differentiating each individual chakra?
As it relates to your specific psychic gifts, what energies did you see, experience or feel?

MEDITATION: CLEARING THE BRIDGE—CHAKRA CLEAN OUT

Become more familiar with your chakras and challenges from the previous meditation. You receive an even deeper healing when you progress through the following meditation. Review the key points:

- Are you familiar with where each chakra is located?
- Do you feel a better sense as to the basic function of each chakra?

- Did you journal the energies around your own challenges associated with each chakra?

If yes, continue onward. If not, take a moment to review the last section.

The key to this meditation is you clear the energy of the challenges you uncovered, i.e. "the dirt" from each chakra. Thus, you are clearing the bridge between your body and spirit worlds.

(Would you rather listen to guided chakra meditations? Visit the Chakra Awakening Course for in-depth training)

Meditation:
(Est. time: 45-60 minutes)
Close your eyes, breathe, be in the center of your head, and with a sense of amusement, give yourself a fresh grounding cord. It's okay to open and close your eyes so you can refer back and forth to the text.

Give a silent "hello" to your 1st chakra.
Notice what energies you sense there.
What stuck or foreign energies might be there?
Notice if there is any "dirt" on the window that is each chakra for the body and the spirit.
You may see it as dark spots, or a static white or grey energy.
You may feel heaviness, lack of movement, or stuckness.
Old memories ready to be released may arise.

Take a clean-out rose. With lots of amusement, imagine the rose collecting up all these energies, vacuuming these energies out.
Explode the rose.
Repeat as needed.

Fill in this chakra in with a mini golden sun.

Repeat the above steps for the 2nd chakra and so on.
Take your time with this.

Once you've filled in each chakra with golden sun, check in with
your body:
Do you feel lighter?
What's shifted?
How's your energy level?

Fill yourself in with a golden sun, stretch, and come out of the
trance

Journal your experience and observations

Working with chakras is advanced work. When you are new to working at this energy level, you may need extra assistance with the healing work. The chakras course mentioned in this chapter is now available online.

It can't be overstated how working on your energy at this advanced level can shift your being. Some students report feeling a need to rest or sleep after a healing like this. Others feel the opposite—they feel alive and full of energy!

In either case, be sure to do some self-care: Drink water, eat organic foods, or take a reflective walk before continuing. Be sure to *ground* even more. Fill yourself up and really replenish your space with lots and lots of gold.

Feel free to repeat this exercise as often as you wish. The experience gets more and more profound each time. You start to gain more access to and even enhance your psychic abilities. You have access to even higher spiritual energies.

Great job! You have worked on clearing the "windows" that are your chakras. Next, we want to give one chakra extra special attention before continuing onto using your gifts to read.

Continue onto the next chapter to find out which chakra. This is STEP 6: Learn how to "raise your vibration" and how to keep your vibration high.

CHAPTER 9 – STEP 6: OWNING YOUR CROWN CHAKRA

KEITH COMES IN FOR HIS NEXT COACHING SESSION. He is a therapist who is quite intelligent and analytical. The challenge with Keith is he may be *too* smart! With him, he learns more to trust his intuition rather than think about it too much. When Keith comes in, he experiences energetic challenges commonly seen at this point of the training.

"I'm starting to feel this pressure around my head whenever I start doing these exercises," says client Keith. "Especially after the chakras meditation, a ton of energy has opened up. Overall, I feel better than ever. But it feels like the pressure is some kind of stuck energy. I've had this pressure since we started a few weeks ago, actually."

"Where do you feel it the most?" I ask.

"On top of my head, especially near the back."

I take a clairvoyant look. "It appears your crown chakra is blocked. It is also quite open. It's more open than usual. You'll want to watch for when the crown is too open like that.

"Because it's so open, I see this white energy on top of your head. It appears like the white is kind of a protection energy. Additionally, this white contains the energy of subconscious thoughts.

"Subconscious thoughts are subconscious for a reason, you know? Sometimes they're buried deep till you are ready to become conscious of them; sometimes they're associated with trauma or bad memories.

"As I mentioned in past sessions, they're more coming to the forefront now because you're ready to release these energies. It's a sign you are ready to take your next steps. It might not feel comfortable. Yet, how often have we had to overcome challenges that were actually *comfortable*?"

"Yes, I can relate," he says. "In my practice with my clients, often dealing with the next level of consciousness isn't always pretty!"

"Yes. I agree. There's a parallel between the work we do. It's no surprise, then, that you can actually *feel* this as pressure near the top of your head. As you know by now, these energies can manifest into physical symptoms.

"As I mentioned last week, we are going to work on the crown chakra. You did your homework exploring the chakras, right?"

"I sure did!"

"Ok, I'll do a quick healing on your crown chakra. Then let's get started."

"Oh, thank you!"

A SPIRITUAL DOORWAY

Mid-way through the Clairvoyant program, there is a new saying I like to introduce:

"When you own your crown, you own your space."

This makes more sense when you imagine your crown chakra as a doorway. As you might have seen for yourself in the last chapter, the crown chakra sits right on top of the head. You might see it as a mini funnel, a camera lens, or an energy ball like I see it. There is no right or wrong.

Since the crown chakra is right on top of the head, below the crown is the body; above the crown is the vast world of Spirit. NOTE: I use the word "spirit" with a little "s" to describe the spirit within you. When I use "Spirit" with the big "S", I am pointing to the whole Spiritual realm.

Imagine for a moment this doorway being open to anything and everything. What would you experience if this spiritual doorway was open to all and any energies out there in the world of Spirit? How would life be for you to be completely open like this?

This explains why many of you report experiencing overwhelm. You experience being over-burdened by your psychic senses. It's too much energy entering your space. It's too much energy entering too quickly. Your crown chakra is *too* open.

In the case of Keith at the beginning of this chapter, this is certainly the case. Especially when it comes to beings and other energies, you must "own" this doorway. Otherwise, it *can be a free-for-all for energies to come and go into your space.*

ENERGIES TO OWN YOUR CROWN

Reread the last sentence in the previous section. When I teach my clairvoyant classes, I get so many light bulbs going off. This is especially true for the highly-sensitive.

The next question always arises, "So, Joe, how do I own my crown? I NEED this!"

Before we get into the spiritual mechanics, I want to introduce to you to a couple more energies. These energies are *essential* to the discussion of owning your crown:

AMUSEMENT

Chapter 5 covers "The Power of Amusement". In each meditation thus far, you work with this energy. This energy helps to not take this work too seriously. When you're too serious, this psychic stuff doesn't work. Plain and simple.

CERTAINTY

The energy of certainty is about the energy of moving forward boldly. It is similar to confidence, yet I want to make a key distinction. In order to be certain, you don't necessarily need to be confident. For example, you can be certain you want to travel down a new life path in your life (e.g. going to college far away from home). Does it always mean you are confident when you get there? Not always.

I'm emphasizing this a bit more because many students feel like they have to be confident first before proceeding with using their gifts. This is exactly *not* what I am saying. Here's the difference: Confidence results because of direct life experience from practicing over and over again. Certainty results from making a bold choice to move forward, even if you have no experience. Children move boldly with certainty into the unknown all the time! Be like a child!

Feel the energy of that for a moment.

The *energy* of certainty helps you be more un-questioning when it comes to your psychic senses. Imagine using a protection rose and not being in a place of certainty of it working.

Like amusement, if you're not *being* certain, this psychic stuff won't work either.

NEUTRALITY

This energy is often the most misunderstood. Often students mistaken this for being "boring" or being like a "doormat". This couldn't be further from the truth! When being neutral comes from a powerful place of choice, then there is nothing boring about that.

For example, imagine meeting a famous Hollywood actor or an iconic hero of yours. Now imagine *not* being neutral upon meeting this person. You'd flip out! Now imagine being totally neutral. You'd very matter of factually say, "Oh you're tall, you have nice teeth, and you have nice bone structure." In other words, you're more in a place to simply see Truth for what it really is! If you are not neutral, then this psychic stuff for sure won't work.

MEDITATION: SETTING THE CROWN TO AMUSEMENT, CERTAINTY AND NEUTRALITY

So how do we own our crown, and therefore own our space? In this meditation, you learn to own your crown. Set it to one of the vibrations covered in the last section: Amusement, Certainty, or Neutrality.

Meditation:
(Est. time: 15-20 minutes)

Close your eyes, breathe, be in the center of your head, and with a sense of amusement, give yourself a fresh grounding cord. It's okay to open and close your eyes so you can refer back and forth to the text.

Run a clean-out rose through your crown to clear any stuck or foreign energies to start. Explode that rose.

Put up a rose in front of you. Imagine this rose is vibrating at the energy of Amusement.
You can imagine an amusement park, a time you had lots of fun, or a funny YouTube video.
What does this rose look like? Is it big?
What color is it? Pink? Cotton candy blue?
If you don't see a color, what is your sense of the energy of amusement?

Take this rose with your psychic hand. And like a magic wand, imagine touching this Amusement rose to the top of your head, the crown chakra.

Have the top of your head vibrate at this amusement vibration for about one whole minute. Notice how your experience is being at amusement.

Open your eyes. Stand up and walk around with your crown chakra set to amusement.

Repeat the above steps for the energy of Certainty, then Neutrality.

Repeat the above steps. This time, set your crown chakra to all three at the same time: Amusement, Certainty and Neutrality.

BONUS: Repeat the above steps. Play with setting your crown to the different colors of the rainbow. Experience how each color feels, one at a time. End with gold.

Run a clean-out rose through your crown and explode the rose. Set your crown to a color or vibration of your choice. You can never go wrong with gold.

With your crown set at this color or vibration, fill in your space with a golden sun.

Take a deep breath, stretch out, and come out of trance.

Journal your experience and observations.

RAISING YOUR VIBRATION

There is a second half to the statement I share with my students, "When you own your crown, you own your space." The second half goes like this: "To own your crown, you set your crown to a vibration or a color of your choice."

When you *choose* to set your crown to a vibration of your choice, you thus set the energy for your doorway to Spirit. In this regard, you allow what you want to come in or out.

You are in control.

Have you ever heard of the phrase, "raise your vibration"? Owning your crown helps you to shift your energy. You have instant keys to adjusting your vibration how you wish.

MEDITATION: RAISING YOUR VIBRATION

In this exercise, you learn to work with different vibrations. If you ever are in a bad mood, you can play with this meditation to elevate your mood. In future chapters, you want to keep your vibration high. Practice this skill for when we start encountering higher spiritual energies.

Meditation:
(Est. time: 5-10 minutes)
Close your eyes, breathe, be in the center of your head, and with a sense of amusement, give yourself a fresh grounding cord. It's okay to open and close your eyes so you can refer back and forth to the text.

Imagine setting your crown chakra at gold. You can create a gold rose and touch it to your crown like a magic wand if that helps. How does that feel to the body?

Now imagine setting the rest of your body to be an exact match at that gold.
Fill in every cell of your body and the rest of your chakras to match that same gold. How does that feel to the body?

Next, imagine your crown chakra at a deep chocolate or coffee brown.
Brown is a lower and slower vibration.
Have you body, your cells and your chakras be at a match.
How does that feel to the body?
A little slower? Maybe calmer?

Now imagine your crown chakra back at gold again.
Since you are working with a higher frequency than brown, you are literally raising your vibration.

How does being at gold feel in comparison to being at brown?

How quickly were you able to switch—or raise your vibration?

BONUS: Play with the vibrations of different elevated emotions such as joy, peace, gratitude and love. The key is to play and not to force anything. Simply be at these vibrations and allow for the experience to unfold.

Run a clean-out rose through your crown and explode the rose. Set your crown to a color or vibration of your choice. You can never go wrong with gold.

With your crown set at this color or vibration, fill in your space with a golden sun.

Take a deep breath, stretch out, and come out of trance.

Journal your experience and observations.

Practice owning your crown chakra in this way each day. Along with using the other tools in this book, your life can't help but to transform!

You are now ready to perform your first psychic reading using your natural psychic gifts! Continue onto the next chapter—with certainty—to get started. We're off to STEP 7: Perform a basic psychic reading using your natural abilities.

CHAPTER 10 – STEP 7: ACTIVATE YOUR 3RD EYE TO READ ENERGY

TEACH A PSYCHIC DEVELOPMENT ONLINE WORKSHOP called, "Awaken Your Psychic Gifts in 7 Days Challenge" where I teach the basic tools found in this book. This mini-bootcamp is always fun to teach. Imagine a group full of novices playing with energy for the first time. As you can relate, many are more psychic than they let themselves believe!

On the DAY 4 of this Breakthrough Bootcamp, I lead them through a fun exercise. The goal is to start clairvoyantly "seeing energy" with your eyes closed. Here's usually how it plays out:

"So today, you are going to see energy with your eyes closed." I say playfully during the live Q&A.

You can *feel* the nervous energy from the group watching this broadcast.

"We're going to read energy?" types one brave soul in the chat.

"Yes!" I exclaim, keeping up the energy of amusement for the crowd.

"Don't worry, the steps you've taken thus far in the pre-training and the last 3 days of this bootcamp up to this point have all been preparation for you to see energy.

"First you learned to ground. This helps you be connected to the planet so that when you deal with energies, your body feels safe.

"Next, you're in the center of your head, a nice neutral space. You know you are neutral because you let everyone else's energies out of that space. You can see things through that 'clear window' now.

"You put up a protection rose to define the edge of your aura and to help you define your space. If the energy of the person you are reading comes your way, that person's energy goes into the protection rose. It doesn't go into your space.

"You then filled in with a golden sun. In so doing, you have a clearer sense of what is your energy and what is not your energy.

"Finally, for extra measure, you set your crown chakra to the vibration of amusement, certainty, or neutrality.

"You are now in a perfect place to give a reading.

"Does this make sense to all of you?"

You can feel the sign of relief...

"Oh wait, what? We've been preparing for it all along?" pops up a question in the online chat window.

"Yes!" I reply.

"And so, before we take the next steps to activate the 3rd eye so you can read energy, I want you to imagine what's your role is as a reader. Close your eyes and imagine a stage. Imagine you are in the audience. The play starts. You see the actors come on stage. The set design shifts from scene to scene. You hear the actors act out their lines. You can sense the energy from your seat as a dramatic scene plays out.

By Joe Gacoscos

"As the audience member, you have no expectations. You're not sitting there trying to control how the actors act. You simply sit back and allow the action to unfold. You're simply the observer of what's coming, going and unfolding."

I have my bootcamp audience open their eyes. "This is exactly how it is with a reading. You prep yourself with the tools. Then from the center of your head, you allow whatever energies you sense to flow. From there, you just report what you see. You're like a news reporter!

"If you see a blue cow walking across the road, report that's what you see! If you hear the voice of an angel say, 'Fear not', you report exactly what you hear. If you get this energy that is not your energy, and intuitively, you get that this energy means, 'watch out,' you report that message!

"When you are completely neutral and in the vibration of certainty, you're simply a reporter. You're matter-of-fact. You tell things as you see them. And you are so completely free of any kind of judgement or bias that you don't put any kind of filter or personal interpretation.

"A blue cow is a blue cow. No more. No less. Even if it makes no sense to you, you report it as you see it.

"**The key point,**" I tell the students, "**to understand is this: Because of how you set your space up with the tools, just have it be that whatever you sense is no accident.**

"**Consider that what you sense, even if it makes no sense at all to you, is what the Universe *intended* for you to see, feel, or hear.**

"So in this sense, you really can't go wrong. Even if it means reporting seeing some non-sensical blue cow!

"Are you ready?" I smile.

People type in, "Yes. Let's go!"

"Great! So let's get ready, close your eyes, and let's get started."

AN ACT OF SENIORITY

Before we continue, you may be wondering why activating your psychic 3rd eye is important. To respond to that, it's at this point, I introduce a new energy vibration: **seniority**.

Many students first find me because they are being controlled by their psychic abilities. Imagine now, you can go beyond being controlled by your abilities. Instead, now you are in control. You are beyond any energies of control. This is what the vibration of Seniority is all about.

Seniority is more than just mastery. You can be senior without being a master. Said another way, you may still be learning about how to own your space. You may not have mastered all the tools thus far. However, you can still claim ownership—or seniority— over your space. You don't have to wait for mastery. You can claim seniority NOW.

Consider all the tools you've learned up to this point in the book. You are much more senior in your space compared to when you first started. **And because the book has set you up to read with all the tools thus far, reading therefore IS an act of seniority**.

Play with it. Have fun! Seniority over your own space is your birthright. It's one of the joys of practicing this work!

As in the "7-Day Awaken Your Psychic Gifts in Days Challenge" story at the beginning of this chapter, each of the previous six steps has been all been a set up to read and activate your psychic 3rd eye.

While some need the extra assistance, most are able read just fine. If they can, so can you! If you're only reading this book, you won't get the same feedback they do because I am not there with you. However, the following steps should set you up just fine to give someone a reading.

(If you do want the extra feedback and training to activate your psychic 3rd eye, learn more here).

Now, remember *amusement?* Let's get started!

ACTIVATING AND READING WITH YOUR PSYCHIC 3RD EYE

I have a surprise for you...

By following along in all the exercises thus far, you are already reading with your psychic 3rd eye!

"How?" you might ask. When you reflect back to the exercises, essentially you are reading yourself. When you see a green grounding cord, you use your third eye to see it! When you picture a stuck dark purple energy in one of your chakras, you're reading with your third eye. When you see a rose explode and burst into millions of pieces, your third eye helps you see that.

You are already using your psychic 3rd eye to read. You are now ready to take the next step and give a reading to others. Being the sensitive psychic you are, you are always reading your family and friends anyway. You are just not reading formally.

Have fun with this. Find a willing friend or family member who is willing to play. Let them know you are just practicing. You are not going for perfect. This is more about practicing amusement, play and seniority.

WHEN YOU'RE DONE WITH A READING

I have one more item to discuss before we get into how to give a reading. Let's talk about what to do at the *end* of each reading. At the of the reading, you want to make sure you don't still have the other person connected to you. You also do not want their energies to remain in your space. When the reading is done, you want to make sure you make complete <u>separations</u>.

What this means is you give them their energy back. You also make sure you get your own energy back. Imagine it's like hanging up a telephone. The goal is you don't stay connected. You freely go your separate ways.

This part of the reading is called "making separations". At the end of each reading, I recommend you make separations and do a complete clean-out of your space. This is a form of good spiritual hygiene.

EXERCISE: ACTIVATING AND GIVING A 3RD EYE PSYCHIC READING

Follow along below to give a reading. NOTE: While you read, you may very well feel a strong buzzing or even pressure in that space where your 3rd eye is located right between your brow. Just know that that's NORMAL! Whether you actually feel anything in your 3rd eye or not, just know that the act of doing this meditation IS activating your 3rd eye.

I can't say this enough: Have fun with this!

SETUP

Find a willing friend or family member. Preferably you want someone open-minded and willing to have some fun with this. Sit across facing each other.

Reader (you): Uncross everything including your arms, feet flat on the floor, sitting up straight.

Readee (the person you're reading): Ask them to sit back and relax. Tell them you will have your eyes closed.

Let them know that what they can expect is you are like a reporter: You will just report whatever energy you see, even if it makes no sense at all.

Remember, there are no accidents the Universe is having you see what you are seeing. You set yourself up using the tools.

Since your eyes will be closed for this reading, you can have your partner read the steps verbatim to you.

Later, you will have this memorized the more you practice reading.

GIVING THE READING

Close your eyes, breathe, be in the center of your head, and with a sense of amusement, give yourself a fresh grounding cord.

Bring your crown chakra to the vibration of Amusement. See or sense it as a color to own your crown. You can also use Certainty, Neutrality, or Seniority if one of those vibrations call to you.

Put your protection rose up at the edge of your aura.

Get a sense of the other person's unique vibration by asking them to say their full name three times.

As the readee says his/her name, you sense their energy.
What color pops into your mind's eye?
Ask yourself, "If I were to visualize this person's energy, how would their energy be represented as a color?"
Take a pause to allow a color to come through.
When some kind of color comes through, this means you are tuned into their energy.

Once you get a sense of their energy, ask yourself the following question:
"What is the brightest color in this person's aura?"
Tune into their unique vibration once again.
Notice what energy comes up. Again, there are no accidents and what you are sensing is what's there for you to sense.

You may see a flash of color. You might see the word of the color, for example, the word "blue" or "green" or "purple".
You might get a feel for a color, or even hear the name of the color.

Go with the first thing that comes to your awareness.
Like an empty stage, have the color come into your field of awareness.
If you sense multiple colors, go with the brightest.
If you are having a hard time sensing any kind of color or vibration, explode roses for any energies of effort. Clear any energies that create a "dirty window" so you can see or sense better. Come back to a place of amusement.

Report to the readee what color you see or sense.

Once you settle on a color, now ask yourself, "What does this color or vibration mean for this person?"

Tune into your own intuition to allow an answer or a message to come through. Again, there are no accidents this is the message you are getting.

Examples:

You may see a bright yellow. You can report, "I get that the bright yellow means she is in a good place in her life. She is happy and content."

You may see a deep royal purple. You can say to yourself, "it looks like the deep purple means she is in a more spiritual place in her life. It seems like she's on some kind of spiritual journey."

If you are having a hard time getting any kind of message, explode roses for any energies of effort. Clear any energies that create a "dirty window" so you can see or get a better sense of the message that wants to come through. Come back to a place of amusement.

Report to the readee your intuitive message.

MAKE SEPARATIONS

See a rose to call your energy back. Explode the rose and watch your energy return to you.

Use a rose to clean your space of the readee's energy. Explode the rose and watch that person's energy return to him/her.

Fill your readee in with a golden sun.

Fill yourself in with a golden sun.

Stretch, come out of the trance.

Talk with your partner about the reading. Gain any validation with what came up in the reading.

Journal your observations and experience.

BONUS: Practice on multiple people to work your third eye seeing muscles.

Congratulations! You gave a reading and activated your 3rd eye in the process! Furthermore, congratulations on gaining a new level of seniority about your psychic space.

As noted earlier, you notice the steps to make separations at the end of a reading. This is important because you don't want to go home still connected to the reading. You don't want to have that other person's energies in your space. You want to keep your space clean.

Ready to take it to the next level still? Now that you have given a reading, you can also give someone a simple healing. Ask if your friend wants to stick around. You'll learn how to give a simple healing next!

Find out more with STEP 8: Perform a karma-free healing without giving away your life force energy.

By Joe Gacoscos

CHAPTER 11 – STEP 8: HEALING "KARMA-FREE" WITHOUT GIVING AWAY YOUR ENERGY

What does "karma" mean, exactly? How often have you heard the following?:

"Oh it's your karma if you do something bad!"

"You'll have bad karma if you do that."

"Karma points for doing the right thing."

For a moment, let's toss all that out the window, shall we?

KARMA: A SIMPLE DEFINITION

Instead, here is a simple definition: **Karma is a cycle.** Like any cycle, there is a beginning. There is an end. Picture a tin can rolling downhill. It starts rolling at the top of the hill. It stops at the bottom. The cycle occurs from when it starts to when it stops. Once there is no more hill, there is no more rolling. Cycle is complete.

The statements above of "good karma" or "bad karma" have some merit to them. However, they miss an important point: When thought of as simply a cycle, then karma is *neither* good nor bad. It's not a curse as some would have it. And just as easily as you can *start* a cycle, you can *complete* a cycle. With awareness—and the energy tools you've learned thus far—you can complete the energy of any karma.

SPECIAL NOTE ABOUT KARMA AND YOUR PSYCHIC ABILITIES

What I notice for just about all of my students is there is some karma around their abilities. This karma is from some past live(s). In an earlier chapter, I mention how you very well may very well be a "Starseed" or an "Indigo/Cyrstal/Rainbow Child". I see some past-life karma around this as well.

When I take a clairvoyant look at different students who come my way, I see past lives as a psychic, a healer, or some kind of spiritual teacher. Unfortunately, in these lifetime(s), they don't exactly use these abilities for good. This ranges anywhere from using their abilities naively causing harm, to using them for mass destruction.

How does karma tie into this? Going back to defining karma as a cycle, in a past life, you start something with using your abilities. If you do cause harm or destruction in that lifetime, you start something. Then as a soul, you decide that in this lifetime you want to make amends for that. You come into this life to complete that karma.

Perhaps you have a "pull" towards developing your psychic abilities or waking up your third eye? Many of my clients report feeling a strong need to want to help others heal. If this is you, then you might want to consider that you have some past life karma around being a psychic, healer, or spiritual teacher.

Perhaps also consider, you are here in this lifetime to complete what you may have started in previous lives with other people. You are here to take your abilities to the next level. If you are drawn strongly to people—friends, workplaces, teachers, healers—perhaps you have karma to complete with each other by giving each other a healing.

This is why I am called to include this chapter of this book: So you can learn to honor your healing gifts karma-free.

Sound good? Let's continue.

Nissa, a professional psychic, comes in for a coaching session. Nissa recently adds healing in addition to readings to her practice. When she comes in, she shows signs of another classic healer dilemma:

"I feel like my body is shutting down," says Nissa. "When I give healings to my clients, they feel great. However, by the end of the day, especially by the end of the week, I'm done!"

"Tell me," I ask, "what kinds of issues are you facing exactly by the end of the week?"

"When I heal people, I think I am taking on some of their energy. By the end of the week, after working with so many clients, it feels like a mix of all different kinds of energies. Basically, I feel burned out."

She continues, "I don't sleep well. I eat pretty healthy. However, it feels like I've gained weight..."

"Ah," I proclaim. "That's a classic sign, the weight gain."

"How so?" she asks.

"Well, think about it for a moment...You are taking other people's pain, issues or energies from giving them a healing. First of all, those are typically heavier energies. Second, if you are not emptying out those energies, then you are storing them in the body. Hence, weight gain."

"Wow, that makes so much sense!"

"Yes, and on top of this, there's a trap many natural healers like yourself can fall into without proper awareness."

"What's that?"

"Let me ask you this, when you give a healing, how much are you looking for the results of your healing? In other words, how *invested* are you in how they get healed or not?"

"Good question. I hadn't thought about that..."

She continues, "After a healing, I do think about it a lot: Did they get better? How are they now? Was the healing any good?"

"I suspected this was the case," I say. "Here's the deal. When you give a healing, and you are tied to the outcome, in essence you create karma between you and your client.

"Here's a question," I propose. "What if your client doesn't heal in the way you want? What if you have twenty healing clients? What if you were tied to how all twenty clients turned out?"

She let the information sink in.

"I would be stuck, wouldn't I? Like *really* stuck." she says softly.

"And," I add, "it can show up as a physical manifestation; weight gain, feeling sick, feeling sluggish..."

"If they don't get better according to *my* expectations," she says, "then I get stuck, too. That's not what I want at all, nor is it healthy."

"Great. You're letting that sink in," I acknowledge. "How would you like to learn a more 'karma-free' way to heal?"

"That would be awesome!" she proclaims.

"And you can still do what you do in your healing practice naturally," I reassure her. "We'll just tweak it a bit."

"Are you ready for this part of your training?" I ask.

"Yes. Let's do this!" she says excitedly.

YOU ALREADY HAVE THE TOOLS TO HEAL

Good news! Since you have been following along thus far, you already have all the tools you need to give someone a healing! These include grounding, clean-out roses, exploding roses, and golden suns. You use these tools to give yourself a self-healing and a cleanout. Next, you basically use these tools to help give someone else the same procedure you gave to yourself.

Additionally, in the last chapter, you learn to make separations at the end of the reading. In that exercise, you take your energy back from the reading and give your readee their energy back. By doing this, this helps you to be karma-free from the reading.

Unlike Nissa in the story above, your energy is not tied to the reading or healing. You and your readee go your separate ways. You are not tied to *how* they heal. Your only concern is that you gave the healing. Let God, the Universe, and their body's natural healing take care of the details. You simply move on untied to the healing.

As a reminder from the managing your energy chapter, even if there is a one percent shift or movement in energy, it's still a healing. As you have experienced already, simply exploding a rose causes a shift. So, too, does grounding. Energy moves! Let's move onto helping others shift with a karma-free energy healing.

EXERCISE: GIVING A KARMA-FREE HEALING

Directions: Use the following steps to give someone a healing. As in the previous chapter, call in a friend or family who is willing to have a healing. As always, be in amusement.

(NOTE: This meditation is an expert from the Clairvoyant Third Eye Reading and Healing Program which follows the 3rd Eye Awakening Bootcamp).

SETUP

Find a willing friend or family member, preferably someone open-minded and willing to have some fun with this. Sit across facing each other.

Healer (you): Uncross everything including your arms, feet flat on the floor, sitting up straight.

Healee (the person you're healing): Ask them to sit back and relax. Tell them you will have your eyes closed. What they can expect is you are like a reporter: You will just report whatever energy you sense (see, feel, hear), even if it makes no sense at all.

Remember, there are no accidents the Universe is having you sensing what you are sensing after you set yourself up using the tools.

Since your eyes will be closed for this heading, you can have your partner read the steps verbatim to you. Later, you will have this memorized the more you practice healing.

By Joe Gacoscos

GIVING THE HEALING

Close your eyes, breathe, be in the center of your head, and with a sense of amusement, give yourself a fresh grounding cord.
Bring your crown chakra to the vibration of Amusement. See or sense it as a color to own your crown. You can also use Certainty, Neutrality, or Seniority if one of those vibrations call to you.
Put your protection rose up at the edge of your aura.

Get a sense of the other person's unique vibration by asking them to say their full name three times.
What color pops into your mind's eye?
Ask yourself, "If I were to visualize this person's energy, how would their energy be represented as a color?"
Take a pause to allow a color to come through.
When some kind of color comes through, this means you are tuned into their energy.

Once you get a sense of their energy, ask yourself the following question: "What is the brightest color in this person's aura?"
Tune into their unique vibration once again.
Notice what energy comes up. Again, no accidents that what you are sensing is what's there for you to sense.

You may see a flash of color. You might see the word of the color, for example, the word "blue" or "green" or "purple".
You might see the word for the color, or even hear the name of the color from your higher knowing.

Go with the first thing that comes to your awareness.
Like an empty stage, have the color come into your field of awareness.

If you see multiple colors, go with the brightest.

If you are having a hard time sensing any kind of color or vibration, explode roses for any energies of effort or anything that creates a "dirty window" so you can see or sense better. Come back to a place of amusement.

Report to the healee what color you see or sense.

Now that you get a sense of their energy, get a sense of their aura. Scan the healee's aura for

~ Dark spots, dark versions of any color, e.g. dark blue, dark green

~ Heavy energies

~ White, grey or static energies

~ Other people's energies

Report to the healee what you see or sense. If you get a message about what these energies represent, feel free to share. If not, that is okay. For now, we will only focus on the healing; often the healee already knows anyhow.

Ask the healee, "Would you like a healing on this?"

If "no", honor the healee's wishes. You do not want to create karma by starting something you shouldn't.

If "yes", continue to the next step.

Create a clean-out rose.

With your psychic hand, take the rose. Send the rose to their space to gather up any dark spots, heavy energies, static energies and/or other people's energies.

Intently watch in your mind's eye the energies lifting up and out onto the rose.

Explode the rose.

Report what you see or sense being released or even how you see the energy being collected by the rose.
Most times, all of the energy is released.
Other times, only some of it is released.
On a spirit level, the healee releases what they are ready to release. There is nothing more needed from you as the healer. Don't force anything not ready to be released.

Fill those spots where energy was release with a mini golden sun.
Fill in the healee with an additional golden sun.

MAKE SEPARATIONS TO CLEAR KARMA

See a rose to call your energy back. Explode the rose and watch your energy return to you.
Use a rose to clean your space of the healee's energy. Explode the rose and watch that person's energy return to him/her.
Fill your healee in with one more golden sun.
Fill yourself in with a golden sun.
Stretch, come out of the trance.

Talk with your partner about the heading. Gain any validation with what came up in the healing.
If the healee didn't feel anything, just know the healing happened on the Spirit level regardless. It could be that the healee may report back to you a few days from now of the effects.

Journal your observations and experience.

BONUS: Practice on multiple people to work your healing muscles.

POST-HEALING PERSPECITVES

Congratulations for giving a healing! Furthermore, congratulations on gaining an even higher level of seniority! Healing karma-free puts you a step above many healers out there.

Additionally, congratulations starting your journey to completing any past life karma! Any drive you've had towards being a psychic, healer, or spiritual teacher may start to make more sense. Don't be surprised if from this point onward, people start approaching you for healings—even complete strangers!

Many students report this all the time. What's happening is people you may have karma with from those past lives are now ready to complete karma—or their cycle—with you. Offering them a healing helps to complete that karma.

Now you are starting to sense there is so much more than simply giving a healing. When providing others healing in this way, it becomes more of a multi-dimensional experience. The experience is one that's beneficial for the healee AND for you the healer.

I recommend you take your time with this. Practice a few healings. And remember at the end of each reading, to give yourself a self-healing so your space stays clean.

In the next chapter, we learn about communicating with beings and spirit guides. You have journeyed through all the energy levels of the previous chapters. You're gaining more and more seniority about your space. This means you are more than ready to start communicating with beings and your spirit guides.

Take a nice deep breath and flip to the next chapter to get started! We're onto STEP 9: Learn ways to work with beings, entities, or spirit guides.

CHAPTER 12 – STEP 9: COMMUNICATING WITH YOUR SPIRIT GUIDES

I F NO ONE IS HERE TO SAY, 'an Angel is extra special', are they really extra special?" Lisa asks me. "Or are they extra special only because we say they are?"

Lisa is a talented spiritual teacher. Her particular inquiry still stands out even after all these years.

"The way I see it," Lisa continues, "In the realm of Spirit, we are all pretty much equal. Aren't we?

"And I mean ALL spirits—from Archangels, to Ascended Masters, to alien beings, to even the lowliest of entities."

I let the Truth of that slowly sink in.

"Now granted, beings such as Ascended Masters and Archangels have had multiple incarnations. They've been on a journey of completing karma and learning many multi-dimensional lessons along the way. This is why we like to learn from them and work with them.

"Ascended Masters like Jesus or Buddha—and allow yourself to go beyond any religious beliefs for a moment—had tough lives in human form. Talking about working through whatever karma they worked through! They're just working through karma like you and I are working through karma.

"Now, in that regard, are they really extra special?" she repeats.

"I hadn't thought of it like that," I contemplate. "I always thought they—beings in general—had this super, mystical, higher power kind of a thing. And I had always thought of some beings or even dead people being scary."

"Yes," Lisa says. "That's the issue when people encounter beings. We give our seniority away when there is absolutely no need. They're just like us. They have personalities and karma to work out just like we do. The difference is we have a body and they don't".

She concludes, "Here's what's to remember: They're only special because we make them special. This is an act of seniority to realize this. Got it?"

"Got it," I say, still letting that sink in.

A PRIMER ON BEINGS WITHOUT BODIES

I debated whether to include this chapter or not. It can be such a charged topic. It can be a scary topic. For many of you picking up this book, beings are REAL. Some of them are indeed scary. And because fear energy is a lower vibration, it can knock you out of your amusement and psychic space. It's because of these very real challenges that I decide to include this chapter.

This chapter is less about the different types of beings out there. Many of you already communicate with guardian angels, spirit guides, or Ascended Masters. Instead, this chapter is more dedicated to being *senior* and how to communicate with beings. This also includes being senior to all kinds of of energies you might encounter for that matter. As we go, I will refer to beings, spirit guides, entities interchangeably. In essence, they're all beings without a physical body.

One note about being senior: Being senior does not mean being domineering. Being domineering is a whole different vibration altogether. We're not trying to dominate anything. Being senior means we are claiming our own space, our own universe.

Being senior is like being a homeowner. If someone rings on the doorbell, you can invite who you want in. You keep out who you don't want. You set the rules for if they get to smoke in your home or not. NO ONE–including beings–can tell you how to run your own home.

Makes sense?

Before we move on, remember what energy level I suggest over and over again? Yes, AMUSEMENT. Bring lots of amusement energy with a dash of *seniority* to your crown chakras right now, and let's continue.

OWNING THE ROOM

Before working with beings, let's take owning your space to the next level. Thus far, you learn to own your aura. Within your aura is your body and your chakras. Next, let's consider the physical room you are in.

When it comes to "owning the room", we are going to use similar tools that we use for managing your own energy. Before we get into how to own a room, I have a client named Trisha who has her challenges with beings. She is a stay-at-home mom. She has challenges with spirits wanting her to deliver messages to their living relatives. This is a life-long struggle dealing with these beings. This story illustrates the before and after when it comes to owning the room she's in.

"Joe, the door is closing by itself," client Trisha's voice trembles over the phone. "It's happening again with these beings."

"That's fine," I state from a place of seniority and neutrality. "Just use your usual tools, own your crown chakra for a moment, and set it to gold. See if you can bring in a higher vibration of amusement as well.

"Gold is a nice high vibration. I find some of these lower vibrational beings don't like gold because it is too high for them.

"And remember, when you own your crown, you own your space. Got it? Plus, I'm here to coach you along so everything will be fine."

"Yes," she says as she takes a big breath.

"I'm going to take you through an exercise called 'Owning the Room'. Are you ready?"

"Yes."

Even over the phone, I could *feel* her eyes watching that door.

"Close your eyes for a moment," I continue. "Now imagine giving your whole room a grounding cord. If you have a square shaped room, imagine that a square shaped grounding cord extends down from the room, all the way down to the center of the planet."

"Ok," she says.

"Whatever energies are in your room, just allow them to slide down this grounding cord."

I take a clairvoyant look. "I'm helping you as well. It's looking good."

"Next," I continue, "imagine setting all the walls and the ceiling to gold. Notice how the energy of your room shifts and changes."

"Ok...wow," she says more calmly.

"Finally, give a silent 'hello' to all eight corners of your room. Imagine golden lines extending from each of them. These are one-way lines from the four corners of the ceiling. One-way lines extend from the four corners below. Imagine that all eight lines meet in the middle to form a big golden sun.

"Great. Now imagine also giving that golden sun a grounding cord extending all the way down to the center of the planet. Down, down, down. And anchor it to the planet."

"Take a deep breath for a moment. And just have it be that if there are any beings in your room, that they are now to be on the outside of the boundaries of the golden walls. Either that, or they slide down the room's grounding cord.

"Declare silently, 'This is my room'."

A long pause...

"Joe..." she says. "It's quiet."

Fighting back tears, she continues, "It hasn't been this quiet around me in a long time."

MEDITATION: OWNING THE ROOM

As with Trisha, she has tried all her life to deal with the beings. What if instead trying to deal with the beings, you were to work on *the space* the beings come in on? In doing so, you create a signal to the Spirit realm that there is a "no vacancy" sign posted for your space. The beings simply go elsewhere.

By Joe Gacoscos

Before we get to communicating with beings, we start with owning the room. This helps to create a clean space. We want to move any other energies out and remove any uninvited guests!

Use the following meditation for whenever you work with beings. Use whenever you mediate in general!

Meditation:
(Est. time: 5-10 minutes)
Close your eyes, breathe, be in the center of your head, and with a sense of amusement, give yourself a fresh grounding cord. It's okay to open and close your eyes so you can refer back and forth to the text.

Bring your crown chakra to the vibration of Amusement. See or sense it as a color to own your crown. You can also use Certainty, Neutrality, or Seniority if one of those vibrations call to you.

Put your protection rose up at the edge of your aura.

Give a neutral, silent "hello" to the energy of your room. Notice the current vibration.
Notice any foreign energies in the space...
Any energies from pasts guests – with or without bodies.
Any heavier or static energies.

Create a golden grounding cord the shape of your room, extending down to the center of Mother Earth.
Like dirty water draining down a sink, watch, feel, experience any foreign or heavy energies drain away. Have Mother Earth recycle those energies for you.
Notice the energy shifts in the room.

JOURNEY OF THE AWAKENED PSYCHIC

Set all the walls and ceiling to gold. Allow anything other than gold to slide down the room's grounding cord. Have your room be a bright 24-carat gold vibration.
Notice the energy shifts in the room.

Imagine one-way gold lines extending from all 8 corners of the room. Watch them meet in the middle to form a large golden sun. Give the sun a grounding cord anchored all the way down to the center of the planet.
Allow any other foreign, dark, heavy, static energies to continue to drain away.

From a place of seniority and amusement, silently declare to yourself, the room, and to any other beings, "My Room".

Imagine any beings now either simply floating away, or being on the other side of your golden walls.

Explode roses in the middle of your room for extra clearing as needed.
See a big golden sun above your room and fill up your room.

See a big golden sun for yourself, fill yourself in.
Take a deep breath, stretch out, come out of trance.

Notice your room with your eyes open, the feel, and the vibration of the room compared to when you first started.

Journal your observations and experience.

PREPARATION FOR GIVING A "HELLO" TO SPIRIT

Setting the room you are in to a nice high vibration sets the proper stage for communicating with spirit. In the next exercise, you will call in one of your helpful spirit guides or a guardian angel.

As with the previous reading and healing exercises, here are a few key points:

- Set your crown to amusement, seniority and/or neutrality.
- Have it be that whatever you might see, sense, hear, or feel in the moment that it is no accident that you are sensing it that way.
- Remember: These beings are special only if we make them special. What if you were to treat them like your neighbor down the street? Or your trusted best friend?
- When you meet your spirit guide, remember they want learn as much from you as much as you can learn from them.
- Lastly, and most importantly, you have the body. These beings don't. You can move through space and time because you have a body. They can't do that unless you *agree* to help them. Without your agreement, they are unable to experience the physical world like we do.

(NOTE: This meditation is an expert from the Clairvoyant Third Eye Reading and Healing Program which follows the 3rd Eye Awakening Bootcamp).

MEDITATION: GIVING A "HELLO" TO YOUR SPIRIT GUIDE

Meditation
(Est. time: 20-30 minutes)

JOURNEY OF THE AWAKENED PSYCHIC

Close your eyes, breathe, be in the center of your head, and with a sense of amusement, give yourself a fresh grounding cord. It's okay to open and close your eyes so you can refer back and forth to the text.

Bring your crown chakra to the vibration of Amusement. See or sense it as a color to own your crown. You can also use Certainty, Neutrality, or Seniority if one of those vibrations call to you.
Put your protection rose up at the edge of your aura.

Ground and own the room you are in, setting it to gold.

Create a "platform" rose in outside your aura. It is hard for beings without bodies to be in this dimension without some kind of medium or platform. Imagine that as your spirit guide comes in, this temporary platform is where the being will stand.

Create a "hello" rose: Create a bright gold rose, and see the word "hello" on top. Drop the "hello" into the rose. Send the hello rose off to find one of your helpful spirit guides. Allow the rose to do all the work for you, finding your helpful spirit guide on your behalf. The rose goes to wherever realm or dimension as needed.

Once the connection is made, invite your spirit guide to come stand on the rose in front of you. Like an actor entering an empty stage, allow the energy of your spirit guide to come in. Your spirit guide <u>wants</u> to be with you. This is why they are called spirit guides.

Allow the being to settle onto the rose. Notice the energy of this being.
~ What's your sense of this being?

~ What does it look like?
~ What's the feel of the being?

Get the sense if this is some other being other than a spirit guide? This can happen and often does. Some beings are so excited when they see an opening to the physical realm. They are like a young 4-year-old, "Look at me! Hear me! See me!"

Come back to a place of amusement and seniority.

If a being other than your helpful spirit guide comes in, playfully yet firmly, show the being you mean business about owning your space. Connect that being up to the Source or the Supreme Being by drawing a gold line from the crown chakra of the being up into the heavens. Imagine the gold line being like an elevator, moving the being out of your room, giving it somewhere else to go. Send it to the light.

As needed, repeat the steps of sending a hello rose to call in your actual spirit guide.
Give a silent "hello" to your spirit guide and get a response. Ask your spirit guide to lower it's vibration a bit so you can see or hear it better as needed.

Start having a conversation with your spirit guide as you would with a being with a body. You can ask things such as
~ What's your name?
~ How do we know each other?
~ What's your job in the world of spirit?
~ How did you come to be my spirit guide?
~Do we have karma together?

Give your spirit guide a fun assignment. Spirit guides LOVE assignments!
~ Ask them for anything
~ Find you a parking spot
~ Help you set the energy for finding a new job
~ Find you a new love interest! (Be sure to be specific about what you are looking for!)

(Fun fact: Archangel Gabriel is the spirit guide helping me hold space for this book!)

Thank your spirit guide for coming in and that you will continue your relationship over time. Send your spirit guide off. Simply see them floating past the gold walls of your room, and floating back to the realm of Spirit.

See a big golden sun for yourself, fill yourself in.
Take a deep breath, stretch out, come out of trance.

Journal your observations and experience.

POST SPIRIT-GUIDE COMMUNICATIONS PERSPECTIVE

Many students are challenged with that last meditation. Some get it right away which is great. Some don't, which is perfectly fine, too! Often there is a lot of religious programming or fear energy that gets in the way of working with spirit in general.

Rest assured, however, these beings without bodies want to work with someone who does have a body! The more senior you become in your space, the more you will eventually be in communication with your guides. With "owning the room" alone, you have a powerful tool to set the stage for communicating with guides anytime.

If you didn't "get it", don't sweat it! Keep practicing the tools laid out in this book. Visit MyPsychicAwakening.com for advanced training options.

Regardless of where you are with your spirit guide communications, you are ready for STEP 10 of the *Journey of the Awakened Psychic.*

The next chapter is a bonus add-on. We take a slight detour from reading, healing, and communicating with Spirit. We move onto the energy of manifesting using our psychic gifts. This step is a great way to cap off the 10 steps of the awakening psychic. Flip the page for how to use the tools you've learned thus far to manifest your dreams into reality.

Finally, here's STEP 10: BONUS ADD-ON: Elevate your energy work with psychic manifestation tools.

CHAPTER 13 – STEP 10: MANIFESTING & GETTING BEYOND "THE SECRET"

M ANY YEARS AGO, THE MOVIE *The Secret* came out. The movie is itself a revelation to millions of people. It teaches in a beautiful way The Law of Attraction. According to Wikipedia.com, the Law of Attraction is defined as follows:

> *"...the Law of Attraction is the belief that by focusing on positive or negative thoughts, people can bring positive or negative experiences into their life. The belief is based on the idea that people and their thoughts are both made from pure energy, and that through the process of like energy attracting like energy a person can improve their own health, wealth, and personal relationships."*

In other words, think more positive thoughts, and more positive things or circumstances come to you. Vice versa, think more negative thoughts, then more negative things will come to you. Easy, right? A whole generation of people chanting millions of mantras of positive thoughts would disagree with you. There is a huge flaw to this Law which I reveal to you in a moment.

Why am I including this as the last of the 10 Steps on our journey? The reason is simple:

You are now at the stage where you can now integrate all the energy tools learned in this book to actually help make the Law of Attraction work for you. You have the tools to make your dreams come true.

This is a great way to complete your journey through the 10 steps. Follow along in the next story where I use a "mock-up" to find a new chihuahua.

"I would like a new chihuahua to be a companion for my girl Chihuahua, Layla," I think to myself many years ago.

"I want this new chihuahua to be at least six months old, a boy, white in color, less than ten pounds, and well-behaved. Most importantly, he has to get along with Layla."

I do my mock-up meditation and I send the mock-up to the Universe. I then go about my daily business.

As the Universe would have it, I check my email and I see a marketing message from the shelter where I had adopted my cat a year earlier. I think, "Hmm, that's a signal from the Universe!"

I check out their website. I scroll halfway down the page. What do I see? A picture of a boy chihuahua, white in color, six pounds, seven months old, and available!

Layla and I hop in the car to drive to the shelter.

As we go towards where this dog is kept, the rest of the dogs start barking as Layla and I walk past.

"These dogs really want our attention," I think to myself. I give them each mini-healing with a grounding cord and a golden sun as I walk by.

We walk to the front of his cage. What do we see? A boy chihuahua, white in color, no more than six pounds, seven months old—and of all the dogs barking at Layla and I, he stands there calmly, looking at me longingly with his puppy dog eyes.

"That checks off the 'well-behaved' box!" I proclaim silently to myself.

This dog, who I would later name Ivan, gets along just fine with Layla in the meet-and-greet session. The next day, I take him home.

As we are driving home, I think to myself, "Wow, I love mock-ups. I mocked it up, and two days later, I come home with the perfect dog. Thanks Universe!"

PITFALLS TO THE LAW OF ATTRACTION

When I look at the Law of Attraction clairvoyantly, here's what I see: Yes, I do see the energies of all the positive thoughts people are repeating to themselves over and over again. However, like a floating iceberg, the positive thoughts are all there above the surface. When looking beneath the surface, what do I see? I see the energies of all the unresolved negative thoughts and feelings lurking underneath!

Said another way, while the Universe is looking at all of your positive thoughts, the Universe still sees the negative energies hidden underneath.

Going back to the iceberg analogy, what's beneath the surface is usually 3x's as much as what is at the surface. In this case, it's a whole mountain of unresolved negativities.

With a mountain of negative thoughts and emotions still present, guess what the Universe delivers to you? At best, you get mixed results. More often than not, you get zilch. The Universe is *confused* as to what you really want.

What else is missing with the Law of Attraction? Sure you are thinking positive thoughts. However, how do you want to *feel*? How would it feel as if you had your dream come true NOW? Would you feel ecstatic? Grateful? In love?

We spend too much time waiting to feel good. We wait till we get that *thing* in order to feel good. What if you were to send a clear signal to the Universe by feeling good now? Feeling gratitude, love, peace, or whatever is the intended outcome?

In the meditation that follows, you learn to overcome the pitfalls of the Law of Attraction so you manifest what you want more clearly.

MOCK-UPS

At Intuitive Insights School of Intuition, we learn all about mock-ups. What is a mock-up? Imagine an artist commissioned to paint a large mural on the side of a three-story building. Before going to paint on the wall, he sketches a "mock-up" on a piece of paper first. Once he is clear on his mock-up, then he goes about painting it on the building.

Now, take a moment to consider your dreams. What would you like to mock up? In my story above, I mock up a boy chihuahua, under ten pounds, white, well-behaved, and gets along well with my other chihuahua, Layla. Some of the other mock-ups I have manifested: A two-seater convertible, a new affordable condo, even this book! The sky's the limit. I say, dream away!

As in my story above with Ivan, you notice how specific I am. This is because we want to send a clear signal for yourself and to the Universe—no confusing signals!

SIDENOTE: As I'm writing and editing this book, I am feeling into how it would feel *now*, as if this book is already complete. I feel excited and such a huge sense of relief!

In the following meditation, you learn to be really clear with your mock-up using all the energy tools you have learned thus far. Read on to discover how (hint: It goes beyond just positive thinking).

MEDITATION: MOCK-UPS

Directions: Use the following steps to create a mock-up. For this particular meditation, I guide you to integrate the contents of this book more fully into your life. Consider for yourself:

- What do you want for yourself and your life?
- What obstacles do you have yet to overcome?
- Where have you been stuck?
- What dreams do you have for your future?
- What is pulling at you with regards to your abilities? Perhaps you may want to start your own healing business.
- How do you want to feel?

Make note of whatever comes up. For now, choose just ONE item to work on. Remember the sky's the limit. What's more important is to be clear so the Universe knows what you actually want. This mediation guides you through that process:

By Joe Gacoscos

Close your eyes, breathe, be in the center of your head, and with a sense of amusement, give yourself a fresh grounding cord. It's okay to open and close your eyes so you can refer back and forth to the text.

Bring your crown chakra to the vibration of Amusement. See or sense it as a color to own your crown. You can also use Certainty, Neutrality, or Seniority if one of those vibrations call to you.
Put your protection rose up at the edge of your aura.
Ground and own the room you are in, setting it to gold.

Create a large golden bubble out in front of you. This bubble will be your "mock-up bubble". It is a space to hold your creation.
See yourself as clearly as possible, as is you are seeing yourself <u>in present time</u>, in the middle of the bubble. Imagine ALREADY being, doing or having your mock-up.

Who are you being? What emotions are you feeling?
Amusement?
Excitement?
Joy?
Profound Love?
Gratitude?

What do you hear? Smell? Feel?
Who's around you?

See yourself in this mock up bubble vividly playing out this mock-up in present time like a movie playing out. <u>Sense this in vivid detail with all your senses.</u>

If you have a spirit guide, call that spirit guide to be on the outside of the bubble. Ask the spirit guide to help you hold and support the space for this mock up. Ask for extra resources. Ask for extra information you haven't considered.

Give the bubble a grounding cord. Ground and drain away anything that's not bright. Ground any dark colors. Ground out any static energy. Ground other people's opinions about your dreams. Ground any energies of past failures if this is similar to a past mock-up. Ground out the energies of any negative thoughts.

Watch your mock-up bubble and all the contents start to become brighter and bolder. The more energy that's released, the brighter and bolder the mock-up becomes.

Explode a few roses around your mock-up bubble for any other foreign energies or any energies not in present time.

Fill in your mock-up bubble with a golden sun.

Draw a gold line from the top of the bubble, all the way up to the Supreme Being. This can be God, the Universe, Source, or whatever fits your belief system. Present this bubble to the Universe, as if to say, "God, this is what I am up to for my next steps."
Get the acknowledgement from the Supreme Being, as if the Supreme Being is saying "Yes" directly in response. You may hear a response. You may see gold sprinkles come down into your bubble. You may get the sense of a blessing from Source. You may receive a symbol providing you more information.

Next, focus on that version of <u>you</u> in the bubble. Imagine now that you can <u>feel</u> how that version of you feels. How are you walking? Talking? Carrying yourself? Speaking with others? How are you sitting? How's the mind of that version of you?

<u>*FEEL the rhythm of that version of you now*</u>*. Imagine walking, talking, carrying yourself, speaking, sitting, running, etc. as that version of you in your physical body.*
Once you feel into that, come back to your own space, your own physical body with that energy. Allow the feel of it to continue vibrating into your own body. Feel it down to your bones. Feel it in your DNA.

Take a DEEP Breath.

At this point, it's important to not be attached to the outcomes. Cut off the mock-up bubble's grounding cord. Release the gold line to the Source. Like a helium balloon floating up into the sky, allow the bubble to drift to the edge of the Universe where all is created. Surrender your mock-up to the infinite Universal Mind. Watch and get a sense of the mock-up as it weaves itself into space and time.

Your job from now on is to just go about your daily life, be in vibrational harmony with your mockup, and pay attention to signs of your mock-up manifesting.

They'll likely show up sooner than you think!

See a big golden sun for yourself, fill yourself in.
Take a deep breath, stretch out, come out of trance.

Journal your observations and experience. Journal any additional messaging from your spirit guide or Source.

Great work! And congratulations on making your way through the 10 Steps of *Journey of the Awakened Psychic*! Making your way through the 10 steps is no small feat!

In the next chapter, you will learn what challenges most clients and students run into while going through this amazing journey of honing and awakening your psychic abilities. Read about extra resources and how you can overcome these challenges.

By Joe Gacoscos

CHAPTER 14 – AM I REALLY DOING THIS RIGHT?

Marie comes in for one of her last coaching sessions. She has come a long way. She starts off being completely scared of beings and entities. She practices the tools daily with plenty of amusement. And she goes from fear to embracing her newfound seniority. It really is a proud celebration of how for she's come on her journey!

That's not to say, however, it hasn't had its hiccups. Even though she's nearing the end of her training, she hits what is called a "growth period". Read on to see if you can relate to Marie's journey:

"At this point in my journey, I feel like I've come a long way towards working on my energy and managing my space," says Marie. "Things are starting to open up more. However, it seems there's something much deeper going on. It feels like something is *off*."

"Great!" I say. "At this stage, let's first of all validate how far you have come compared to when you first started. That's a triumph!

"Second, realize this isn't exactly a linear journey. Some days you'll feel great from all the release of energy. Other days, you might feel just out of it. This is because your body is still trying to catch up to the changes."

"Body is trying to catch up? Can you say more about that?" she asks.

"I'm happy to...We're all spirts on a journey this lifetime, living in this vessel we call a body, would you agree?"

"Yes. It's definitely been a spiritual kind of a journey when you put it that way."

"Yes, and those parts—the spirit and the body—are both important. The issue is that spirit understands or gets this information quickly. Spirt has no bounds. Spirt can literally travel across Universes in an instant if it wants to.

"On the flipside," I continue, "there's also the body. Unlike spirit, the mind and the body move and vibrate at a MUCH slower pace. So while your spirit moves quickly, the body needs time to catch up.

"That catch up period is what we call a 'growth period'...

"It's like riding a roller coaster. The roller coaster ride itself may last no more than 2 minutes. However, 20-30 minutes later, your body might still be reeling from the rush of the ride! Even though it's exciting, the body can feel off. It feels disoriented. It takes a bit to recover, even if the ride itself was quite exciting.

"Does that analogy make sense?"

"I feel that way sometimes. I feel great, especially right after a healing. However, I feel off a few days later. Is this a sign I'm in a growth period?" asks Marie.

"Yes. A lot of times you might feel blocked." I respond. "You might say to yourself, 'this psychic stuff isn't working'. Or you might feel something deeper going on as you had stated earlier.

"Other signs and symptoms: You might actually feel sluggish or tired. You may feel a deep need to simply just relax. You might in general feel *off*.

"What's import to realize during these growth periods is this is not a *bad* thing. It might not feel great going through a growth period. Yet, realize that going through a growth period means you are making some serious strides in your psychic and spiritual work.

"Does that make sense? This is all the nature of spiritual growth; it's like layers of an onion. You've only scratched the surface."

"Ah, that makes so much sense. So basically, nothing's wrong with why I'm feeling off. It's just the nature of spiritual awakening. Got it!

"So what's next? I've learned all these cool new tools. Where do we go from here?"

"Great. Let's talk about that right now."

GROWTH PERIODS

Life is all about shifting and changing. We decide to take a bold step. We try things out. We reevaluate. Then we take the next steps. That's the linear approach. In reality, life can be more like a roller coaster. You go up to the highest highs! Down to the lowest lows. Sometimes you go where your heart leads you. Other times, you end up with regret not taking a chance. Ah, life!

Many clients and students liken their journey through the *10 Steps* to a wild psychic journey. Others report their experience as having gone through 10 years of therapy in 10 weeks. Others just feel like a different person altogether.

As in the client story above with Maria, what you are going through is what's called a "growth period". A growth period is one where:

- You go through the material in this book, and who you are as a *spirit* gets it very quickly
- You experience the steps of the meditation exercises, and your spirit is gleeful with joy.
- Your spirit is already jumping ahead to what's next? What's next? WHAT'S NEXT?!?
- While that is great for spirit, there's the body. The body vibrates much slower.
- While spirit may be twenty steps ahead, the body is still relatively slowly... feeling... things... out.
- The body needs time to catch up!
- The catch up time *is* the growth period
- While going through the "catch-up" period, you may feel <u>misaligned</u>
- You may feel like your abilities "aren't working"

WHAT A GROWTH PERIOD IS NOT

It's important to acknowledge that it's *not* that your psychic abilities aren't working. Like the dirty window analogy, a clear window is always underneath; it's just that it's covered up with dirt. Going through the layers of your spiritual journey is just like that. Just when you think you have it all together, the next insight, or the next level of growth is waiting for you. Many times it's right around the corner. It can appear like dirt. Underneath, however, is even more of the clarity you've been longing for.

In this regard, while a growth period might not feel good in the moment, growth periods are a good thing.

It's important that you not give up in moments like these on <u>any</u> life challenge you undertake. You are simply going through a growth period. Understand that the catch-up period can be anywhere from days to weeks at times. This depends on the amount of energy you shifted.

ENERGY CHECKS: INSIGHTS INTO WHAT YOU DON'T SEE

Like anything in life, when you are too close to the action, you can easily be blind to the obvious. Going through a growth period is exactly that. There may be some deep core energy lurking underneath that you are unaware of. You sense something is there, and yet you can't quite pinpoint it. You don't know what you don't know, right? **While all this is normal, you need <u>not</u> remain stuck without answers**.

When I work with my clients going through a growth period, often what I find is there is an issue with their tools. What I look for in this specific type of reading is to see how their energy is flowing or not. This particular reading is what's called an "energy check".

For example, I check your grounding cord.

- Is your grounding cord wide enough?
- Are there blocks?
- Are there hidden energies that block your energy from flowing?

Or I check your chakras:

- Are your chakras in harmony? Balanced?
- Is one of your chakras not spinning properly?
- Is a blocked chakra causing physical manifestations like pain? Tension?

Once the issues and blocks are identified, just as you learned in this book, I can easily give you a healing.

Check in with yourself now. How are you feeling? Any sluggishness? Uncertainty? A feeling like a deeper core energy is there you can't quite pinpoint? Feel like you need some relief and clarity? Might there be an old being in your space?

Before you decide something's wrong with your abilities, what's likely going on is you need an energy check. The energy check will help you move past energy blocks both seen and unseen.

Overcoming these blocks is easier than you think. Schedule an energy check at https://www.mypsychicawakening.com/reading-healing-sessions/.

AM I DOING THIS RIGHT?

The most common question I get when it comes to developing psychic abilities is this: **"Am I doing this right?"**

I get it. It's like the chicken and the egg scenario. I include the energy of Certainty in this book. It's easy for me to say, "Be certain". However, unless you have the feedback, it's hard to be certain. It's hard to know if you are doing this right in the first place in order to be more certain.

What are students *really* seeking? **Validation**. Validation goes deeper than "yes, you're doing the right thing." When I speak of validation, I speak of feeling the answers all the way deep down to your very core. It's getting past block to your Truth I speak of in the Prelude of this book.

In the beginning of the book, I also mention the "knowing about" trap. Where most students get stuck is where they tell themselves, "I already know about all this. I still don't know why it's not working."

This is where a trusted guide comes in. The guide helps you understand the "why" of "why it's not working." When you work with a guide who has been there, done that, and has overcome similar challenges you are facing, this is a great mentor to have in your corner.

Rest assured, you have all you need with the steps laid out in this book to

- Control your psychic abilities
- Own your space
- Give a reading and a healing
- Manifest with psychic tools

While you can do all the above on your own, what's missing of course is individualized feedback. Like many of the client stories in this book, it's great when there is someone credible and experienced to guide you. This guidance ensures even greater chances for your spiritual success.

SUPPORT FROM AN EXPERIENCED MENTOR

Every budding psychic should have a mentor. Mentoring provides two things: VALIDATION and ACCOUNTABILITY. As you journey through this book, you are likely asking these questions:

- Am I doing this right?
- What do I do next?

- What am I supposed to focusing on?
- What am I supposed to be seeing or sensing?
- What does *that* mean?

Validation from an experienced mentor answers these questions.

Additionally, anyone on a psychic journey will at one point encounter a challenging energy along the way. When challenges arise, I find people generally fall into two camps: They convince themselves they must keep going no matter what. Or, they justify why it's okay to give up. They say to themselves "I'm fine" when clearly, they are suffering. Why does this happen? I find it's because they have no structures in place to keep them accountable. No one is saying, "Don't give up on your dreams!" For this reason, accountability is equally as important as validation on the psychic awakening journey.

What do many students do when they encounter an especially challenging energy? Sadly, some quit. Many give into fear. Ironically, overcoming these challenges are handled in a single coaching session call. Even more sad, often on the other side of breaking through these barriers is the pot of gold mentioned in the chapter entitled "Uncovering a Buried Treasure".

Validation and accountability help ensure that you don't quit. You remain empowered to keep leveling up with your awakening. You see what's beyond the veil.

HOW TO FIND A GREAT MENTOR

Personally, I've invested an almost embarrassing amount of money on training and mentoring. As mentioned before, when I go for something, I tend to go all out! That said, I know investing in mentoring is a big decision. Compared to years of being stuck, however, I find choosing mentoring to get me unstuck has always been the better choice.

Having worked with many mentors—some great, some not so great—I want to pass onto you what to look for when searching for a mentor. I recommend finding the BEST mentor out there who has what I call the "rare trifecta". Here are the three elements of the trifecta:

1. Reading and healing abilities
2. Spiritual wisdom
3. Teaching mastery

Many are great at one or two. However, being great at all three is the rare exception. The last quality, teaching mastery, is especially hard to find. The other two, spiritual wisdom and reading and healing abilities are more common in the psychic community.

When you "click" with a potential mentor, I recommend you do what it takes to work with him or her. Especially when you intuitively have a deeper spiritual connection with this person, you should consider working with this teacher. Remember the chapter on past-life karma? Perhaps the Universe brought you and your mentor together for a reason. Ever hear of the saying, "When the student is ready, the right teacher comes along?" I'm constantly amazed at how true this is.

YOU ARE SUPPORTED

Many of you have been dealing with your psychic challenges all your lives. How much longer will you keep dealing with these challenges? What's it costing you? Your family? Your careers? Or your relationships to stay stuck in this situation? How long will keep delaying the inevitable—that your gifts are calling on you to awaken to your true spiritual path? Perhaps you are that next great spiritual healer, reader or teacher?

I encourage you to come out of hiding in the shadows. The world is waiting for you to shine your light. If there is even a slightest pull to explore receiving mentorship, it is a pull worth exploring.

Likewise, if you feel a pull to want to work with me personally, consider that that's why this book *found you*. Flip to the "Supplemental Materials" at the back of the book for a listing of coaching and e-courses for more information. Remember that you get an exclusive access to the "Awaken Your Psychic Gifts in 7 Days Challenge". You can get full access at a reader-only-discount using coupon code MYAWAKENING.

For those who want to continue their 3rd eye awakening even further, there's the full **Elevate Your Psychic Gifts Reading and Healing Program** which you learn more about on the last day of the Awaken Your Psychic Gifts in 7 Days Challenge.

No matter which route you take, just know you are not alone. If anything, be sure to join our growing community on Facebook. Know you are supported. There are many like you on a similar journey.

By having gone through the steps, you are officially on a new path to making the most of your gifts. It really is an honor for me to have walked with you this far on your journey. Before we wrap this up officially, flip to the next chapter for a cosmic vision for what you can expect next for yourself, your communities, and even the planet.

CHAPTER 15 – A WHOLE NEW WORLD AWAITS

As mentioned in the chapter about beings, Archangel Gabriel has been on the ride with us. She (or he depending on your perspective) is who I've turned to to help hold space for writing this book. She is a messenger angel who will continue helping you the reader should you wish for more of her help.

Archangel Gabriel would like to share her message with you. Here is her unedited message:

A CHANNELED MESSAGE FROM ARCHANGEL GABRIEL

"You are a master of your domain. Right now, your domain is simply still unknown to you. How do you know what's your domain? You're sitting in it, right now, right where you are.

Where you are is perfect. Your life is no accident. You are a star, one of the millions and billions you see as you look up at the night sky. You are already part of the cosmos. You matter.

You are part of the whole and yet, you have a unique gift, ready and waiting to be shared. Share that gift now. Share that gift soon.

The world awaits."

A CHANNELED MESSAGE FROM A PLEIADIAN BEING OF LIGHT

At the end of any of the programs I teach, the following question always comes up: "What's next?" To answer that question, I'd like to share a quote from a reading I received a few months before writing this book. This message was channeled to me from a Pleiadean being of light. The message has since been a compass for me whenever I consider what are my own next steps. As you read this quote, I invite you to get what resonates with you as you consider your next steps:

"A diamond is one of the most beautiful stones in existence. You hold it up to the light, and it shimmers and sparkles unlike any other substance. What you see, however, is the finished product.

What you don't see is where the diamond comes from. Miners dive layers and layers to the most dangerous depths of the Earth to find these diamonds. Sadly, some people die trying to excavate these diamonds.

Still, once the diamond is discovered, it is only a diamond in the rough. There is still much work to do to polish it to its exquisite best.

This is how people are, Joe. They are miners searching the depths of their Souls for the Truth. They search for the meaning of life, for the meaning of their existence. Throughout the ages, people have given their lives in their quest for finding true meaning in their lives.

What you provide, giving these blessed souls the gift of psychic sight, is you help people to excavate in a different way. Rather than dig through danger, you help people peer past their tough layers, and give access to their deepest depths...

In essence, you help people get connected to those hidden depths. These depths they may otherwise never access without their abilities.

Do you see what a gift that is?

The gift of psychic sight is not your gift to hide, Joe. It is your gift to share with others, so they then can help others discover their own diamonds in the rough. And then those people can help others. And then those people can help even more.

By sharing your light, do you see what a world this could be?"

A VIEW FROM THE COSMOS

With that, realize your psychic gifts are part of some greater cosmic purpose on your soul's journey. With where the planet is at today, the world needs more people like you to shine their light. There's nothing wrong with bringing more healing to the world, right? You are a light warrior with a gift to share. You may not have a desire to become a professional healer. Yet, there are plenty of other ways to heal.

Be inspired to share your gifts. When you do, I promise you, what returns to you is greater than what you can even imagine right now.

And remember, you already are a diamond, ready for the sparkle of your light to give healing to others.

Never dim your light. May your light always shine bright.

Many blessings to you,

Joe

By Joe Gacoscos

CLOSING REMARKS

ACKNOWLEDGEMENTS

T HIS BOOK IDEA IS INSPIRED by the many students who came through my classes while teaching at Intuitive Insights School of Intuition, located in San Diego. Each and every single week, I watched them gain higher and higher levels of awareness. The transformation over the months of training was truly a beautiful sight to behold. I am grateful and honored to have been a part of your spiritual journeys.

This book is also inspired by the many reading and healing clients. These are brave souls who took that first step to transform their lives. As you transformed, so too did I. It's an honor to be part of your journey.

Many thanks go to my teachers, coaches and mentors, those who helped me acknowledge my own "diamond in the rough", who encourage me to push the boundaries of my psychic abilities: Jenny Knowles, Vessa Rinehart-Phillips, Katherine Schiff, Cody Edner, Lisa Davis, Kristyn Caetano, and many others with and without bodies including spirit guides, healing masters, angels, Akashic record keeper, and intergalactic councils of light.

Lastly, many thanks to my family. My dad, Onofre Gacoscos, who taught me to just go and do it, not take things so seriously; my mom, Pat Gacoscos, who never stopped loving and supporting no matter what; my sister, Rosella Garcia; who always supported my wildest out-there endeavors; and my beautiful nieces and nephew, Izzy, Zenaida and Ian, who inspire me to be the best example I can be.

ABOUT THE AUTHOR

JOE HAS GUIDED HUNDREDS of awakening intuitives break past barriers to honing and embracing their psychic gifts. He provides worldwide students and clients spiritual tools for healing, self-discovery, clarity of mind, and soul-aligned living, causing a massive shift of consciousness on the planet and beyond.

He teaches clairvoyance, awakening the 3rd eye, and connecting with angels and spirit guides. As a spiritual teacher, he helps awakening psychics, Starseeds, empaths, and the highly sensitive hone their psychic and spiritual gifts. As a gifted healer and psychic, he has helped his clients reconnect to their higher calling, and realign with their soul's true purpose.

Joe is founder of My Psychic Awakening Academy. Visit MyPsychicAwakening.com for more courses including the "Awaken Your Psychic Gifts in 7 Days Challenge", the Clairvoyant Training program, and healing support for this book.

SUPPLEMENTAL MATERIALS

BELOW ARE RESOURCES for one-on-one mentoring and home study courses as mentioned in the book. Click on each link or visit the website for **My Psychic Awakening Academy** at MyPsychicAwakening.com for in-depth descriptions.

7-DAY ONLINE PSYCHIC DEVELOPMENT TRAINING CLASSES
Awaken Your Psychic Gifts in 7 Days Challenge
https://my.journeyoftheawakenedpsychic.com

ELEVATE YOUR PSYCHIC GIFTS MEMBERSHIP PROGRAM
Beyond Awakening: The Opportunity to Elevate Your Psychic Gifts Presentation
https://www.mypsychicawakening.com/elevate

SCHEDULE A PSYCHIC READING & HEALING
Energy check
Chakra Healing
https://www.mypsychicawakening.com/reading-healing-sessions

THANKS FOR READING

THANK YOU FOR READING *Journey of the Awakened Psychic*. Many who have come to embody the steps outlined in the book are astounded by how transformed their lives have become.

I created companion programs for this book which can be found over at MyPsychicAwakening.com. If you want to find out more about how to awaken your psychic abilities, check out the training. Let me know what you think. Connect with me on your favorite social media platform.

May you have a blessed journey ahead!

Joe Gacoscos

LET'S CONNECT

Facebook

https://www.mypsychicawakening.com/secret-group

Instagram

https://www.instagram.com/joegacoscos

YouTube

https://www.youtube.com/c/MyPsychicAwakeningAcademy

Made in the USA
Coppell, TX
22 December 2023

26801897R00111